A Place to Be

Praise for *A Place to Be*

"*A Place to Be* is a wonderful book, beautifully written, with vignettes and moving reflections on places ranging from Afghanistan to Armenia, Burkina Faso to Madison, Wisconsin. It is also a timely book, given ... the positive impact made by committed foreign service officers like Cheema who represented the U.S. in difficult circumstances while also making a difference in the lives of others."

–Jonathan Addleton, US Ambassador, retired; rector/president, Forman Christian College, Lahore, Pakistan

"JK Cheema's *A Place to Be* is the fascinating story of a remarkable life spent all over the world. It's honest and thoughtful, rich with wisdom about everything from being a woman in the workplace to the patience and bravery required to bring slow, incremental change to the world."

–Michelle Wildgen, author of *Wine People*

"*A Place To Be* comes at just the right moment as USAID and other government departments are being dismantled. In this highly personal memoir, Dr. Cheema takes us inside the workings of US AID, describing the idealism and the hope of our teams around the world; the life-altering (and often life-saving) contributions they made in the areas of health, education, economic development, disaster relief, and security in countries around the world; and most importantly how US AID's 'soft power' cemented partnerships, making the United States safer and more secure. If you want to understand what we have lost and what we need to rebuild, read this riveting book.

–US Ambassador Marie Yovanovitch (ret), author of the best-selling diplomatic memoir *Lessons from the Edge*

"Virginia Woolf once said: "As a woman I have no country. As a woman I want no country. As a woman, my country is the whole world." The issue of belonging and home resonate through Jatinder Cheema's fascinating memoir *A Place to Be*. From a young girl witnessing the violence of partition in her native India, to eventually becoming a senior foreign service officer with USAID, Cheema has documented 'how systems turn against their own people'—particularly against women—and more importantly, how people can endure and even conquer those systems by creating homes for themselves and each other."

–Rita Mae Reese, author of *The Book of Hulga*

Also by the Author

*As I Remember – The Life History of
Raminder Kaur Cheema*

The Black Attaché – Vignettes from a Life

A Place to Be

Vignettes from a Life

JK Cheema

CALUMET EDITIONS
Minneapolis

Contents

Part I: Making a Life – Making a Difference 1
Part II: Exploring the World 117
Part III: Being a Woman 181
Part IV: Home 227
Acknowledgements 245
About the Author 247

CALUMET EDITIONS

Minneapolis

First Edition 2025
A Place to Be: Vignettes from a Life
Copyright © 2025 by Jatinder Kaur Cheema.
All rights reserved.

No parts of this book may be used or reproduced by any means, graphic, electronic, or mechanical, including photocopying, recording, taping or by any information storage retrieval system, without the written permission of the publisher except in the case of brief quotations embodied in critical articles and reviews.

Printed in the United States of America.
10 9 8 7 6 5 4 3 2 1
ISBN: 978-1-962834-55-1

Cover design by Christopher Chambers
Book design by Gary Lindberg

Ode to My Mother, Raminder Kaur

Who transitioned from this world on 25 October 2023

What is my spirit but my soul
Searching for space.
Wandering and flying, reaching far and beyond
to find silence and peace.
Speak to me my spirit and calm me
So, I can breathe.

Author's Note

This book is not a sequel to my book *The Black Attache – Vignettes from a Life*, but there is a connection. Some sections in this book make references to events which are more detailed in *The Black Attaché*. Although they do not need to be read in sequence, reading both books will give readers a fuller picture of my life.

When I finished *The Black Attaché* three years ago, I was sure I had told my story. However, friends wanted to know more about my work and career. Thus, the first part of this book is in response to my friends' requests. Going over my diaries and journals, I found other stories that I wanted to share. The question of what it is to be a woman in a man's world has always interested me, and likewise the question of home has stayed with me throughout my life as I moved so often.

The first part of this book, "Making a Life—Making a Difference," was the hardest to write. During my career there were so many stories, so many meaningful events and memories. Thus, selecting what to write about and who to mention and give credit to was difficult. I tried to mix work experiences with personal perspective and stories to show that even in some of the most difficult situations, there was hope.

Some names in the book have been changed for privacy purposes.

To My Readers

If you have a story, tell it.

If you are in darkness look around—there is always light through an opening.

If you are sad, use the moment to reflect and learn from your sadness.

If you feel hurt, forgive those who may have hurt you.

If you feel guilty, make amends.

If you are angry, pause and reflect.

If you are uncertain, make a choice—let your choice determine your path.

If you are lonely—reach out and touch someone and say,

Talk to me.

I dedicate this book to all who worked for USAID —the Americans who did their patriotic duty to serve their country, representing us around the world. And to the host country USAID employees who believe in the American values, democracy, and generosity.

PART I

MAKING A LIFE—
MAKING A DIFFERENCE

"You may find that making a difference for others makes the biggest difference in you."

Brian Williams

Introduction

I proudly gave twenty-five years of my life in the service of the United States Government working for the United States Agency for International Development (USAID). For the US government abroad, development is part of the 3-Ds: Diplomacy, Development and Defense. The US government, Republican or Democratic, recognized that the 3-Ds working together are important to achieve our foreign policy goals. The 3-Ds help counter terrorism and the influence of governments that deny their populations free speech, rule of law, and the right to basic needs. The 3-Ds make our shores safer. The work of the 3-Ds protects and promotes the interests of our businesses and safeguards our economic interests overseas. The 3-Ds strengthen US influence abroad as one unit. In my opinion, it made the US presence stronger when negotiating for our interests and values with governments like-minded or hostile. Past administration and congress supported foreign assistance because they understood that a stable world is in our best interest.

USAID was responsible for many of the programs that fell under the Development part of the 3-Ds, funded under the foreign assistance budget approved by Congress. USAID is there when famines displaced people without food or shelter. We are there providing humanitarian assistance in camps where people fled from ethnic violence so they could survive. We are there when there is an epidemic like Ebola, HIV/AIDs, avian flu, and others, to save many from dying abroad and keep the viruses from our borders. We are there in countries with flagging economies, raging unemployment, and poor agriculture sectors to modernize and create jobs, motivating many to stay home as their economy grows. We are there for many in autocratically governed countries, strengthening civil society institutions and media so people can have a voice and be heard. We are also there for our private sector, protecting and creating opportunities for our businesses to expand their markets overseas.

At home, USAID helps our farmers by procuring 40 percent of humanitarian assistance to feed the hungry in the world. We are providing research opportunities and employment for many in the US who worked for the universities, non-government organizations and the private sector agencies implementing USAID programs, because they believe in promoting US interests and helping the world.

In early 2025 as this book was going to press, the current administration closed USAID without due diligence, preparation, or planning, upending the work and the lives of thousands of US citizens and millions of people all over the world.

While I support improving efficiencies and eliminating waste and redundancies in any organization, there are rational and humane ways to do so. The decision to close USAID with no notice was neither. USAID employees work at the will of the US Administration and Congress implementing our foreign policy goals. To label USAID as a criminal or a corrupt organization was wrong.

With USAID closed, many people around the world might die of hunger and disease without the food and drugs that USAID provided. Our HIV/AIDs program saved millions of lives which are now at risk without access to life-saving drugs. Without USAID's disaster relief efforts, many more will be displaced and die. Without USAID work in collaboration with international organizations and the Centers for Disease Control, our borders will be vulnerable to epidemics such as Ebola. Without USAID's work in leveling the playing field and improving transparency in the business environment in other countries, US firms will be disadvantaged.

Without development assistance—or soft power as USAID's work is often referred to—we have lost a voice and influence at the international table. USAID inputs were important to leverage resources from other donors and negotiate cost-effective ways of implementing programs. There are many examples of why foreign assistance and USAID matters in the world and in the US. Now, other countries, especially China and Russia, will take advantage of the vacuum and increase their influence and power. Without development assistance, US foreign policy and influence is weakened.

I understand that USAID work will now be under the State Department and some humanitarian and other programs, yet to be determined, might continue in a limited manner, but a lot of damage has been done and time lost. I am hoping that a course correction will take place and soon some mechanisms are in place to restore the development part of our foreign policy agenda.

Part one of this book is about my experience of my work with USAID. It is about how I got to where I did professionally, what I believed we achieved, and what I learned from my colleagues as a person and a professional. It is about my road to working with USAID. There was so much more in my experience with USAID, many more examples, but I could not cover them all. There were so many people who helped me achieve what I was able to, but I could not cover and mention all of them. I selected what I thought told my story best. My friends and colleagues who worked with me might remember or view some of the situations differently, but these are my personal impressions.

Born into Turmoil

When I was born on July 27, 1942, in Lahore, which is now in Pakistan, my parents could not have imagined that I would one day be a senior executive representing the United States government. Neither my parents nor I could have guessed where our lives would lead and where we would end up.

It was a time of turmoil and uncertainty. World War II was underway. The India independence movement had started. There was talk of separating India into two countries based on religious preferences. Muslims wanted their own country, Pakistan. Sikhs who had lived for generations in Punjab, one of the states that was divided, were nervous about the future, not knowing where the border would be drawn.

I was born at my maternal grandparents' house. As tradition then required, my mother returned to her parents' home to give birth to me. My grandfather worked in the British civil service and was posted in Lahore. Times were politically difficult, but I was told that everyone was happy to have a baby around. My mother was nineteen years old. From what she remembers, I was born at 7:00 a.m.

The Summer of 1947

The summer of 1947 burned in my memory. My mother, my sister, and I were visiting my paternal grandparents for the summer, which was our normal summer routine. My paternal grandparents lived in a village called Wadhai Cheema near the border of what is now Pakistan. During our visit of 1947, my father wanted us to return home early. The independence of a Muslim country separate from India was in full swing and rioting had started. Although officially the border line was not announced, it was rumored that Wadhai Cheema would be in Pakistan. My grandfather accompanied us to the train station. The dirt road to the station was full of people on the move by foot or whatever transport was available to them. People were desperate to get on the trains that were still operating. We were trying to get to Faridkot where my father was the agriculture officer in charge of a research farm. Faridkot was on the Indian side of the newly drawn border. He wanted us back with him as he feared our safety.

My father had sent two bodyguards, one Muslim and one Sikh wearing long swords around their waists to accompany us. I remember being hungry, I remember my sister crying. She was then two years old. I remember being scared. I remember wondering what was happening, but I was afraid to ask. My mother tried to protect us by assuring us that we would be fine. She closed the wooden window shutters to protect us from seeing what was happening outside; but it was too late. I had seen the horror surrounding us as we boarded the train. I saw mothers crying, fathers crying, begging people to take their children on the train. Fear in their eyes as to what might come, as mobs ran around amuck with wielding swords. I wanted my sister to stop crying. I wanted it to be calm, so I could think. I was hungry but afraid to ask for food.

Thanks to the bodyguards we made it to Faridkot alive. Passengers on the next train were not so lucky.

My Early Education

My father was in the civil service and by the time I was six years old, we had moved five times. I enjoyed moving. I liked new adventures. I liked having new kids to play with. My mother tells me I often took the lead when playing and decided what we were going to play and how. As an adult, I find myself managing and organizing and taking charge of decisions when needed, to the annoyance of my siblings.

My formal schooling did not start until I was seven years old. I remember some home schooling and going to a school for a year or so in a small town called Nabha where my father was posted. I learned how to write Urdu and Hindi on a wooden slate before going to an all-English school. My maternal grandfather, close to retirement, was then posted in New Delhi and my parents decided to send me there for schooling. They thought it was better for me to have continuity in my education rather than moving so often from school to school. My grandfather enrolled me in St. Mary's Presentation Convent, then considered to be one of the best schools in North India. I lived with my grandfather, his two sons, a daughter, a daughter-in-law and their kids. My grandmother had died when I was six years old.

St. Mary's was an English language Catholic school. The nuns would not permit us to speak Hindi, the national language, or Punjabi, my local language. Later, the government required that Hindi be taught as a second language as it was declared to be the national language. All classes and subjects were in English, so it became my first language. I think in English. I dream in English, I speak English most of the time, and I write in English. I do wish though that I had retained more of the Hindi, Urdu and Punjabi. I can speak and read a little Hindi and Punjabi.

It was my mother's goal for me to have a good education, possibly because she'd given up her schooling when her mother died. My mother had five younger siblings, and my grandfather took her out of school to help with caretaking. She would later tell me that she would have been a doctor if she could have finished her education. She was determined that I would get the best education possible. Her consistent message to me was that women can do anything men can, and that I should aspire to achieve my goals and to not be afraid. She wanted me and my sister to live our lives in a meaningful way without fearing that we were in some ways handicapped by being women. She was progressive in her thinking. Thus, I grew up aspiring to be independent, to have a career and hopefully make a difference.

I liked reading when I was young. I would read everything in sight, without any parental controls. My grandfather left me pretty much to manage myself. I was lonely and I found solace in reading. I also found being in school difficult. I remember mean boys who used to tease me because I was chubby and had long thick black hair. They loved pulling at my braids. But I fought back. I never cried.

The nuns were strict. I used to rebel against rules I thought were unfair, and I would get the class to follow me. At home, I was pretty much left to do my own thing and make my own rules. If I thought something was not right, I would speak up. At school, I remember the sound of the smack of the ruler on my outstretched palms. I remember standing against the wall at the back of the class with my arms outstretched. But I would not cry even if my arms hurt when I believed I was right. Sometimes I was in the wrong, like leading a group of girls to hide behind the window to the nuns living quarters to see what they wore under the habit or if they had hair. We were often caught.

Some nuns were kind. They gave me treats and lunch sometimes. I am not sure if they thought I was an orphan as my grandfather came to school on Parents' Day and not my parents or felt sorry for me for getting into trouble often. I did enjoy the treats and lunches of baked chicken and potatoes, which were very different from the chapatis and spicy dal and vegetables at home.

I was in awe of the nuns and sometimes wanted to be one. I treasured the small colorful cards they handed out with fairy tale like pictures of Jesus and Mary. I was not sure if I was supposed to accept these cards, so I never showed them to my grandfather.

In school I found myself on several school teams, basketball, hockey, and a game much like volleyball, but called netball. My favorite was basketball. In 1958 my school team won a gold medal in all state championships. My US friends are surprised that at five feet tall, I was on a basketball team. Schools in India then did not have much to choose from as basketball was not as popular with young women as was field hockey and net ball. I continue to be active in sports to this day.

I was also involved in other extracurricular activities. For Independence Day Parade I led the youth scouts' group and marched down the boulevard at India Gate, turning to salute the dignitaries in the VIP box. For the national cultural day, I was selected to perform national dances, wearing colorful clothes. I do not remember my grandfather enrolling me in all these activities, so I must have enlisted myself to participate. I did not want to miss out on anything. He did take me to all the practices though.

I also took music lessons. My grandfather bought me a sitar. I wanted a piano, but we had no place in the house to put one, nor could my grandfather find a teacher. I continued sitar lessons throughout school and college. I took music as a minor in my college and did well playing sitar. I gave it up when I moved to America. Sitar is not an easy instrument to travel with, and I was too busy trying to finish my studies and learn to live in the US. Music then was not my top priority. I went back to taking piano lessons later in my life.

I was a good student in school and got good grades. I knew my mother wanted more from me. I had seen my father and maternal grandfather in the civil service serving people. My paternal grandfather was head of the village and was always working for the wellbeing of the people, as did my grandmother, by helping the women in the village. My mother always wanted us girls to make a difference as she would have if she had finished her education. While in school, I knew that when I grew up, I wanted to work and do something important. Maybe I was touched by humanity when I saw the awful events of the partition when I was six that I wanted to make the world a better place

Thus, when I was about twelve or thirteen, we were at the airport seeing my dad off to Cornell University for his PhD under a Ford Foundation scholarship. I saw him board the PANAM flight to New York, I knew then that I wanted to do the same. I had no idea what a PhD was or what it entailed. I had heard him tell my mother that getting a PhD would help advance his career and he could do more for people and the country. From then on, in my mind, having a PhD became a must if I wanted to make some difference in the world and have a career.

In 1956, my father was posted to Chandigarh, a new city with an acceptable high school. I moved to live with my parents. My experience at the Catholic school had taught me to appreciate discipline and patience, which I needed in a new school with no friends. I was angry at having to move and leave my friends behind, but I also looked forward to being with my parents. I was lonely and had difficulty making new friends in high school where I was a new student from a big city and not welcomed by the small-town high school kids. Looking back, I admit that I did come across a bit arrogant about being from Delhi, the capital of the country. I thought that the kids in the new school were a bit provincial.

I turned to books. Books about the Holocaust interested me the most. Possibly because of the events I witnessed during partition when I was young plus in the news, we would hear about the gas chambers used by the Nazis to kill the Jews. I remained curious how people survive in difficult situations and how systems turn against their own people. I started keeping a journal also, which like reading became a lifelong habit.

I did not play sports in high school. I did not feel that I fit in with the other students. I spent more time studying and topped my class. My mother would have liked me to do more with my friends but reading and my journal entries were enough for me at that time.

Girls College in Chandigarh

By the time I finished high school, Chandigarh did not have many choices for undergraduate studies. There was one college for boys and one for girls. I started my undergraduate work with pre-med classes. Being a doctor seemed to me a good way to make a difference and have a career. However, I could not dissect a rabbit or a rat or any other animal. I would feel their pain even though I knew they were not alive. I gave up on pre-med. My counsellor suggested psychology and sociology. I could be a psychologist if not a doctor, I thought. I elected Music as my minor subject of interest. I had started to enjoy the *Sitar* and was good at it.

My four years in college were somewhat disappointing to my parents. I spent far too much time with friends, too much time going to parties, too much attention on boys, and my grades dropped compared to my performance in school. Personally, I was disillusioned by the Freud school of psychotherapy, which was in vogue at that time. I found it condescending towards woman. I changed my major to Sociology. Throughout the college years, I found myself floundering a bit, not sure what I wanted to do and who I wanted to be.

Except, it was in college that I first became aware of diversity in a different way. India is full of diversity, not only in class and caste, but every state in the country has its own language, culture and traditions and some differences in facial features. But this experience was different.

I had to take a foreign language as a requirement. I elected French. In a mostly all-female teacher's college, Mr. Smith was the only man. He was tall and lanky and walked into the class so casually that I missed his entrance the first time. He wore loose fashionable shirts over his pants. He had long brownish hair, unlike anyone in the neighboring boy's college. We learned that he had lived in France and that he was Anglo-Indian. Anglo-Indian was a label used for kids born from marriages or affairs between Indians, mostly women, and the British, mostly men, who ruled India for a century. Secretly mothers and grandmothers liked the light skin color of the Anglo-Indians, but socially they did not accept them. We girls thought he was handsome and looked forward to his classes. We all had a crush on him.

In the second year, rumors started to spread that he was a homosexual, the term used for gay people then. Something changed. I noticed that many of the girls in the class started to laugh at him when he entered and some of the girls started to play mean pranks, like throwing chalk at him when he turned to write something on the board. It was such childish, teenager like behavior and I did not understand nor agree. When I said something to the girls, they laughed at me. I came home and told my parents about how mean some of the girls were. Some of the parents met with the principal, but I learned later that our handsome French teacher left the collage and moved to another city before the term ended. He had given everyone a passing grade before leaving. I was shocked and angry at how mean and prejudiced people can be, some of them friends of my parents.

The School of Social Work in Delhi

After finishing my bachelor's degree in 1964, I took a break from school and went to Delhi. I struggled to find myself as a woman and a person. I did not want to get married; I wanted a career but had no idea how to go about it. There were not many women role models beyond doctors or teachers. I already knew being a doctor was not for me, and I thought being a teacher was limiting. I wanted more.

I moved away from home and went to live with my grandfather again in Delhi and joined a typing school. My dad, through his contacts with the Ford Foundation, got me a job with the foundation as a receptionist. I was hoping my time off from school would help me find my direction in life. I was also hoping that working for an international organization, such as the Ford Foundation, would broaden my knowledge about future areas of work. And it did. I met and worked with professionals in the areas of health, agriculture, education and learned about how philanthropy works. The year and half at the foundation expanded my network of friends into a wider international community, mostly from the US. I became more interested in international issues.

During my time at the Ford Foundation, I made friends with Karen, a social worker from Berkely. She was taking a year off from work and visiting a friend who worked at the Ford Foundation. With her, I travelled all over India. Until I met Karen, I had no one to travel with and my parents were hesitant to let me travel by myself. I knew that there was so much to see in India and so much that I wanted to know about the country and its different cultures.

Karen had talked a lot about how much she enjoyed being a social worker and how she found the work gratifying. I did some research and discovered that the Delhi School of Social Work had a degree program in psychiatric social work in conjunction with the Chicago School of Social Work. I applied and was accepted. I felt I was back on course a bit.

As part of my social work program, I had to do two internships. During my first internship, I was assigned as a social worker to work in a youth rehabilitation hostel. The boys ranging from the age of ten to fifteen were serving sentences for minor thefts, use of drugs, and some for major crimes, like assault and murder. I was nervous and a little afraid when I started working with them. The kids were mean and tough. The hostel was located up on a hill away from the neighborhood. I walked from the bus stop up the hill everyday questioning—can I do this? The boys at times were hostile and at other times indifferent. It seemed to me that they had given up on having a better life. Many of them were homeless and came to the shelter through the juvenile court system.

I had an office, but in the summer, we held individual and group sessions outdoors under the cooling shade of a tree. I was not an expert in the field yet. I was starting my internship and was still learning how to put theory into practice. The more I learned about the kids' background and their history, the more clearly, I could see how they got to where they did and how best to help them. One of them told me, "If I had one person in my life to guide me or even to tell me that I was going down a bad road, it might have made a difference, but there was no one. I have lived on the streets since I was five. I have been bad ever since to survive."

Listening to their stories was hard for me. I knew that social services had very little budget to help train them to develop skills that might change their lives once they had done their time. I tried to negotiate for whatever I could to get them skills training, like carpentry and plumbing. With the help of the hostel supervisor, we were able to get a carpentry program started. Some kids were beyond my help. Their mental health issues needed a different kind of counselling and support, but the hostel did not have the budget for specialized services. Sadly, I knew that they would go back on the streets and suffer more and get into more trouble, till they ended up in prison for good once out of the juvenile system. I did my best within the limitations of my own skills, as I was still learning the ropes of being a social worker. I listened to them, gave them what counselling I knew best, took their cases and causes to the management, accompanied them on their court dates, made them feel that they had an advocate in me. Over time I think I did make a difference in some small way in their lives. When I completed my internship, a few of the boys cried.

During my second year, I was assigned to a low-income slum area in Delhi to promote maternal healthcare and family planning. The field site was on the outskirts of New Delhi. Each morning, I took the local bus, Number 7. The overcrowded bus provided ample opportunity for men to rub against young women. I had many confrontations with men on that bus that taught me lessons about self-defense. It brought home the fact that as a woman, I had to be on guard.

When I started my internship, I had thought that I would just knock on the door and the women would be happy to see me. I had a good message to deliver, such as good health and family planning to space their children which would reduce the infant death from malnutrition. I was so wrong. This was 1968. I was working in a low-income, mostly uneducated community. The women thought that I had some hidden agenda for promoting fewer children, that I was a foreign agent, or that the government had some reason to target them to have fewer children because they were poor. For the first couple of months, women would turn away when I approached or go into their small houses and shut the door. Or they would shout at me and say, "Who will take care of us, if we do not have children? Go away." I was humiliated and shocked. I had to change my approach.

I stopped knocking on the doors. I would go every day nine to five and just walk up and down the alleys, resting on a chair that I would find outside a house or on a charpoy. If I saw kids playing, I would ask them about their school. After some time, a few younger women finally approached me, and I was careful to keep the conversation on what issues they were dealing with and their needs. Slowly, with patience and time, I won the women over and by the time I finished my internship, I was able to talk about the benefits of spacing children as a health issue both for mothers and children, although talking about family planning and having few children was still a sensitive subject. I learned during that internship that listening, patience and proper messaging suited to the situation was important to succeed in changing behavior.

There were times during these internships that I wanted to quit. I felt helpless and inadequate in my skills and resources that I had to offer. The work was physically demanding and tiring. The voice of my mother—to never give up—kept me going. Besides, what were my options? The aunties were ready to get me married. They were busy trying to get official photographs of me to show to the potential future husbands. If I wanted to be independent to make my own choices in life and have a career that made a difference, I had to finish my degree program.

While at the school of social work, I met Dr. K., a professor working on a behavior change and communication research project funded by the school of public health from a university in the US. He offered me a part time research assistant job. I worked for him on weekends and continued working with him after completing my social work degree. As a result, I started to think about public health as a career. With his help, I applied and was accepted by the Johns Hopkins Public Health doctorate program in Baltimore with a full scholarship. I was thrilled.

A Wrong Turn

And then, I took a wrong turn in my life. I made a bad decision. Just before I was supposed to leave for Baltimore, I got married on the rebound. I had been seeing someone for two years and he left me for another. I was devastated. It was a bad time to make a bad decision. To this day, I cannot explain my reasoning. Maybe I was emotionally vulnerable, maybe I thought I could do both: have a career and get married. Maybe I got cold feet. And maybe there was societal pressure. I was twenty-eight, and an unmarried woman. In India being unmarried at that age meant there was something wrong with her. It might have weakened my resolve.

I had met a man from the US who worked with an international organization in Delhi, and he totally wooed me. He said that I could do anything I wanted after we got married, that I could get my PhD and have a career. I believed him. After we got married, I moved with him to Pakistan and then Sri Lanka where his next assignments took him. The marriage lasted for three years. In 1974, I packed my bags and went to New York where my best friend Karen then was living.

My mother would often ask me why I did not come home to the family. I could not tell her that I was embarrassed. That all my life, I wanted to work and get a PhD and then when the opportunity came, I got married. I felt that I messed up my life and wanted to straighten it before I could go back to India. I also felt that if I went back to India, I would not be able to leave and would drown in the sympathy and judgement from my aunties who would be thinking silently "what do you expect when you marry a foreigner?"

Separation was hard for me. I had made my own decision to get married. With the marriage ending, I began to doubt myself and my decision making. I was hurt and angry and felt betrayed. My trust in marriage shattered. But I knew that living in that relationship would not have been good for me as a person and a woman. However, all did not end up badly where the relationship was concerned. My ex-spouse had two sons from a previous marriage who visited us in Sri Lanka during their school holidays, I bonded with them. Over the years we have maintained contact. We discussed getting together and a bit hesitantly in August 2024, I flew to Arkansas to meet them and their father. We laughed at old stories, and we talked about good and not so good times. We spent hours watching slide shows that the eldest son had put together from our Sri Lanka days. It was like a family reunion. I was touched when the youngest of the two hugged me and said, "I am never going to let you go." I was glad that I made the trip to see them.

My Move to the US

By the time I moved to the US to live, I had my citizenship through marriage. I had visited the States for holidays, but I had never lived there for more than a few weeks at a time. This was going to be a major change for me, and I was both excited and nervous, but motivated to start a new life.

While staying with my friend Karen, I applied to several public health schools. I was accepted into the School of Public Health in Boston and moved to Cambridge. I had applied for a scholarship and was confident that I would get one. I needed a scholarship. Out of pride, I had agreed to a small separation allowance from my ex-spouse. I regretted that later.

I had maintained contact with a friend from my work with the Ford Foundation who lived outside of Boston and knew the city well. He recommended that I find a place in the Italian section of Cambridge Street where rents were affordable. He helped me find a studio between Harvard Square and Beacon Street. The owner had a hardware store on the ground floor. The mother had come to the US as a teenager and the mother and son lived on the second floor and me on the third. The son, Francesco, managed the store, while the mother owned the business. I never saw a father around. I did not know anyone in Cambridge and found myself sitting around the office and talking to Francesco. Everyone knew each other. People from the neighborhood dropped in to Francesco's office all the time to chat, mostly speaking in Italian. Sometimes there were loud exchanges. I wondered if Francesco was in the mafia. He rode a fancy car, had a boat in the harbor and dressed well. He also knew everyone in the neighborhood. Once, a man came in the office and reported that a suitcase had been stolen from the grocery store across the street. Francesco looked at me and said, "Let's go find out who stole it." We got in his car and drove from house to house. He knew where the teenagers lived. We found the suitcase. No one reported anything to the police. I had no idea what was in the suitcase and why it was so important. I became interested in Italy and added it to my bucket list to visit once I had a job.

The mother would give me administrative tasks that also helped me financially. She also fed me with delicious Italian food. My separation allowance from my ex-husband which sounded like a lot when I was in Sri Lanka, but in Boston it was just enough to cover my basic expenses and little to spare for eating out, shopping or entertainment. I did not want to ask for money from my parents. I was nearly thirty-one years old and was embarrassed to ask for help. I learned to live by limited means, and it was a good lesson for me in frugality.

Then, I learned that Boston school did not provide any financial support. I had also applied to the University of Michigan-Ann Arbore School of Public Health, where Dr. K, my professor friend from India taught behavior change and communication courses. I was accepted with a scholarship for tuition and a stipend of four hundred dollars per month for living expenses. The term started in September 1995. I had a couple of months before I needed to move, so I decided to stay in Cambridge. I enjoyed the Italian neighborhood. It reminded me of India, where people just dropped in. Hawkers selling vegetables and fruits would walk their carts in the neighborhood and people came out with their baskets to buy what they needed.

Knowing that finding a job would be difficult for the short time I had left to stay in Cambridge, I decided to volunteer, first at a hospital in the elderly ward for terminally ill patients. I helped feed them and listened to their life stories. Many of them had no families and some had families who seldom visited. I felt sad for them. On weekends, I also volunteered at a home for mentally challenged youth. I would take them on field trips and to the park and conduct group activities as required by the program director.

In my free time, the Italian family took care of me as if I were family. One time in the middle of the night, I heard banging on my door, only to realize that the mother had seen someone climbing up an electric pole to my window. She and Francesco came to check on me. The man saw the commotion and we saw him slide down and run away. Again, no one called the police. I went back to sleep.

My time in Cambridge made me ready to live in the US. I learned how a small, family-owned business is managed, how to survive on limited finances, how the social sector addresses the needs of the elderly and mentally disadvantaged, and above all how to live alone and manage without family and friends. My one friend who lived outside of Boston did see me occasionally to make sure I was doing okay – but other than him, the Italian family became my family and friends. I regret that I did not learn Italian cooking from the mother.

The University of Michigan

I moved to Ann Arbor in August 1975 and found housing at the Ecumenical Center. I shared a two-bedroom apartment with three others. A Japanese woman from Tokyo and a woman from Puerto Rico had come a day before and had taken the larger of the two bedrooms. The other small bedroom was barely big enough for one bed and I was supposed to share it with the fourth roommate, who showed up a day later. We managed to squeeze in a mattress next to one bed, moved one dresser into the living room, and in those close living spaces we became the best of friends. Sandra had moved from Philadelphia for her post graduate work as a psychologist. Living with her I learned about life in the US as a black person and a woman.

My scholarship was for a one-year master's in public health, a shorter program because I already had a master's degree in social work and had completed the core courses. I worked as an associate for one of the professors during my master's program. He knew that I was interested in post graduate work and told me about a scholarships program for minority students under the affirmative action policy. I applied and was delighted to learn that I was accepted into the PhD program through the department of sociology with a scholarship for tuition and a stipend. I felt like I had won the lottery. The affirmative action policy is being revoked or being questioned now throughout the US, but without that assistance, I would not have been where I am today.

After completing the required courses for the PhD program, I submitted a proposal to go to India for my field work research. I developed a framework based on a qualitative model, known as grounded theory. I was more interested in questions such as "what", "how" and "why" of social interaction which a qualitative model addresses better than a quantitative model. I wanted to develop my own theory about human interaction based on my data and observations. I selected a rural agricultural area in the state of Punjab. My proposal would examine how the public sector's services responded to the needs of the people living in villages ranging from lower to upper economic status. I planned to conduct interviews and focus groups to collect data. For the department of sociology, which was a believer of quantitative methodologies as being truly scientific, did not look upon my innovative approach as real research. It took some months justifying my rational and academic thoroughness in conducting my research and collating the information into a cohesive dataset that my proposal was finally approved.

In India, one of my relatives loaned me a Jeep that I drove through dirt roads, visiting and taping interviews with farmers and their families in their homes and during focus groups. My nephew, whose parents were from that area, came along to help me navigate the roads. Each night another cousin helped me transcribe the recorded interviews in a diary. Without their help, I am not sure I would have been able to complete my field work.

On returning to Ann Arbor, I discovered that collecting data was the easiest part. Analyzing it and forming my theory and writing the dissertation was agonizing but challenging. My scholarship was for five years, meaning that I had to complete my dissertations and defend it by the end of 1981. I had enough data for two or more dissertations, my committee chair told me, and that I was making the process far more complex for myself. "Stick to your proposed model and get rid of redundant material." He said. Easier said than done.

What I discovered did not come as a surprise. I found that the public sector was more responsive and worked better for those who were economically better off and knew how to take advantage of the available services. The low income and poor got left behind as they did not know how to navigate the government system and the extension workers, who were supposed to help them, avoided the poorer villages.

I vividly remember the evening when I defended my thesis in December 1981. I managed, with the help of my chair, to get my dissertation committee to meet on the last school day of the year for my defense. The scheduled time was 6:00 to 8:00 p.m. It was a cold Ann Arbor evening, and a snowstorm was predicted. I was ready but extremely nervous. One of the professors from the department of sociology on my defense committee had difficulty accepting the qualitative nature of my dissertation work. During my consultations with him, I would come out crying, sometimes wanting to give up. Looking back now, I think his demands helped me develop research and analytical skills that have benefited me in my career. To this day, I research every topic more than necessary.

The defense involved two hours of rigorous questioning, especially from the difficult professor and it affected my self-confidence. I started to wonder if I would pass. The tone of his questions made me feel like he was questioning my whole thesis. He asked for more evidence to justify my premise and theoretical framework. Then he congratulated me, as did the whole committee. They all got up and left, wishing me and each other a merry Christmas and happy holidays. I was stunned and in shock. For me it was the biggest moment in my life that I had been dreaming about since I was twelve or thirteen. For them it was just another dissertation defense. I left the building alone. It had started to snow. I went for a long walk. I looked up at the falling snow and shouted, "I did it!"

I went to my apartment and called the operator to put a call through to my parents in India to share this moment with them. When I received my certificate, I was pleased to see the words "innovative work" in the paragraph stating that I had obtained my PhD.

Ann Arbor also had an important influence on my thinking and professional growth. I had the opportunity to meet and become part of the inner circle of Professor Henryk Skolimowski, born in Warsaw, who taught philosophy in the department of humanities. He often invited philosophers from other countries and held discussion groups at his house. His thoughts on eco-philosophy and environmental issues opened new ways of thinking about philosophy, life and the environment for me.

Another person in Ann Arbor who solidified my progressive thinking was Rich Ahren, an architect and artist, and a liberal thinker. He lived simply, travelled all over the country in his camper, drawing and sketching historical buildings. His house in Ann Arbor was a welcoming place for protesters, hippies and reformers. I am sure that the government had a record on him for his criticism of the systems and the government. The last time I saw him was in 1983, when he came to Washington, DC, to draw the capital. He had me pose wearing a red *sari* and standing under a tree with the capital building behind me. The print of that sketch hangs in the entry way to my condo.

I found letters and many postcards from both Henryk and Rick in my black attaché. Reading them, I wondered if I had responded with equal interest. I regret not having stayed in touch with them, until it was too late. I had learned so much from knowing them both.

I loved my time in Ann Arbor. I started going to football games and realized that I enjoyed being part of the enthusiasm that surrounds the football season. I participated in Halloween, Christmas and Thanksgiving celebrations. Sharing a room with my Black friend, showed me a side of the US that I would not have easily experienced otherwise. I learned that everything was not as it seems on the surface. Ideologies and deep-rooted belief systems about race and religion were part of the country where I had started to feel at home. The absence of women lecturers in all the departments where I took classes did surprise and bother me.

I made wonderful friends, some, I am close to even now. The 1960s still lingered on the campus. The six years that I spent in Ann Arbor made me think differently. I became aware of social justice and equality in ways I had not thought of while growing up in India. I felt that I had finally arrived at a good place in my life as an independent woman. I got divorced. I was enrolled in the PhD program—my lifelong goal; I had enough money to share an apartment of my own. I felt free to live my life as a woman by my values and belief systems without being judged by culture or family. By the time I finished my studies at Ann Arbor, I felt at home in the US and felt that I belonged.

My Experience as a Consultant

For months prior to my dissertation defense, I had been thinking about the next step: a job. I wanted to do international work. While I was in Michigan, a friend from my master's program joined USAID and helped me get a job with Battelle International, a technical firm that was working on a USAID contract in health policy. The project office was based in Washington, DC, so I moved there in 1982. My friend had rented a two-bedroom house on Q street in Goerge Town, and I moved in with her. I loved living in Georgetown, I could walk to work to my office downtown on M street and enjoyed my walks in the neighborhood admiring the architecture of the old buildings where some of the famous people had lived and still lived.

While at Battelle, I traveled on a needs assessment trip to Sudan during one of the worst droughts in history. I travelled around the countryside and was shocked to see animal carcasses laying around and groups of people on the move to find food. I had read about the famine and seen pictures on television, but the firsthand experience of seeing such dire desperation made me feel sad, and guilty that I was so fortunate. I was pleased to be working with USAID which had saved many lives in Sudan by providing food aid and medicines.

On the last day of our trip, a colleague from the American Embassy invited me for a beer. The hotel in Khartoum was located at the edge where the White and the Blue Nile Rivers meet. After spending fifteen days on the road amongst the worst drought to date, it was surreal to have a beer and watch the two Niles merge and flow peacefully onwards toward Egypt. I wished more countries would work together so peacefully.

I had been with Battelle for a year when they decided to downsize. They had bid on projects that did not materialize. There were rumors that people would be fired and since I was the last to be hired, the probability was high that I would be the first to go. On one Friday, just before the weekend, when most of us would go to happy hour after work, I was called to the director's office and was handed a letter. No warning. I was devastated. There must be better ways to fire people. I thought of suing them and even consulted a lawyer, who advised against it.

From 1983 to 1985, I could not get a full-time job. For the first eight months, I lived on unemployment benefits. I had to move out of the Georgetown house as I could not afford the rent and moved in with a family friend in Arlington who had a large house and plenty of space. She said I could stay with her until I found another job. However, living with her did not work out well and I moved to a studio apartment near Boston metro station.

Living on unemployment taught me again how to live frugally and experience the hardships of being poor. I also realized how easy it would have been for me to enter the world of homelessness during months after unemployment benefits ended, and I had no regular job. I borrowed from friends or sold some jewelry to pay for my rent and food. I tried finding jobs at drug stores and restaurants but was told I was overqualified. I was forty years old with two master's degrees and a PhD and unemployed. I decided that once I found a job, I would never be without a job ever again.

I did find short-term work, but not continuously enough to be able to live comfortably and without worrying about how I would pay my next month's rent. The World Bank hired me to evaluate their health projects in Bangladesh, Indonesia and Thailand. The World Bank assignment was an eye-opener to the systemic shortcomings in the development business. My team found poorly constructed health centers at high costs. At one health center, I scratched a wall with a knife and instead of concrete, I found just sand. Quality materials that were budgeted for were not used. By the time our reports were completed, new projects were already in place and some key findings could not be incorporated. Since then, the World Bank and many other development agencies have undergone reforms to streamline and tighten up monitoring and eliminate loopholes in their systems.

As my World Bank assignment was coming to an end, a colleague, knowing that I needed work, gave me a reference and a contact in United Nations Children's Fund (UNICEF) office in New York. UNICEF had an urgent need for a technical person to help with their evaluation systems. I got a three-month assignment. I stayed in a hotel first and then house sat for a colleague who was on leave for the summer. It was my first time living for an extended period in New York. My mother came to visit me with my three-year-old niece, Sukhmani. While showing them around New York, I discovered the city and fell in love with it.

I was desperate for fulltime work. My friend, Mike Jordan, who was posted in Washington, DC, recommended that I apply to the University Research Corporation (URC), a large firm, that was bidding on a health operations research project for USAID. I met Mike in 1968 when I was in the school of social work in Delhi. He was working for USAID. His wife Betty was a designer. I spent time at their place helping her with tie-dying materials for clothes she designed for fashion shows. I modeled one of her petite jump suits, maroon in color, made from thick cotton mixed with soft wool and studded with small pieces of glass that sparkled in the bright lights of the catwalk. It was my one and only experience at modeling. I kept that jumpsuit for years even though I could not fit into it, finally parting with it when I gave it to her daughter in 2012.

My Work with USAID

Bangladesh

On Mike's recommendation, I agreed to be listed as one of the key staff on URC's proposal as the health technical specialist. There were two other key staff from the US and the senior most with management and research background was listed as the chief of party. By the time USAID awarded the contract, the other two had found jobs, so I was sent to Dhaka, the proposed location for the regional project office. I was asked to take on the role of acting chief of party. I was responsible for getting the office in Dhaka established and getting pilot projects negotiated in Bangladesh, Nepal, Pakistan, Thailand and Sri Lanka.

I was completely unprepared for the job. I was a technical person and had little administrative experience. We were expected to have pilots started within a year. We barely got our Dhaka office functioning and filled the remaining US and local staff positions in the first year. Although I was constantly traveling to negotiate and obtain agreements from the host countries, the project was way behind schedule.

I was excited about the work. The project was designed to improve efficiency and streamline bureaucratic procedures by learning through implementation and continuously improving the delivery of health services in the host countries. The travel schedule and stress of meeting project goals did affect my mental and physical health. I gained twenty pounds living in hotels and being hosted by our counterparts. I overate everywhere. I had been an exercise junkie all my life, but during that year, I hardly went to the gym. I lived in a hotel for the first six months. Finding a house and getting the lease approved from the URC head office in the US took time. I was afraid of losing this job. I did not want to be unemployed again. I made the mistake of not asking for help because I felt I had to prove something and could do it all. I was wrong. All aspects of the project were behind schedule. The USAID Washington project officer was not happy and I was fired.

I was angry, frustrated and thought I had been treated unfairly. However, one incident during my time with the URC was of personal significance to me. I was in Peshawar to meet with government officials. One of the Pakistani officials had the same last name as mine. He did not remember if his grandparents were from the same village as mine as there are two villages of predominantly Cheema families. We started to share stories. I told him that my grandfather had been posted in Peshawar, and I vaguely remembered his house where my sister was born. He immediately suggested we should go look for the house. I got into his vehicle, and we drove to the cantonment area where the government officials lived. I was nervous. I knew I should not have risked being there because the State Department security officer in his briefing was particular about not venturing out in the city. But I could not let the one chance to see the house slip. We drove up and down the street looking for the gates that matched my description. Most of the houses on that street had similar gates, but finally, we stopped in front of one that I thought might be the house.

We parked the car. I slowly got out and stood in front of the locked gate and a host of memories from my childhood flooded my mind. I remembered playing hide and seek and hiding in a trunk in my grandmother's room. I remembered my mother carrying a blanket in which my baby sister was wrapped as she rocked her to sleep. I remember sitting on the floor in the verandah with a large towel under me and eating watermelon out of a bowl. My mother told me that I loved watermelon. Every time a fruit vender came by the gate, I would want more watermelon. My grandmother could never refuse, so I ate and ate watermelon to my heart's content. My kind Pakistani Cheema counterpart offered to help me go to Lahore where I was born and to visit our ancestral village of Wadhai Cheema, but I knew better and thanked him for his kindness.

It is said that when one door closes another opens. One of my colleagues working at USAID/Dhaka office recommended that I should apply for a personal services contract (PSC) position recently opened in the bilateral USAID mission for a health specialist. By then I was familiar with the health issues in the region. I had no other options as I did not want to return to the US and be unemployed. I did apply and was relieved to get the job. I was assigned as the project manager for the family planning program. Assistance for family planning was then one of the largest bilateral funding in the region. The average fertility rate in Bangladesh was one of the highest as was child and maternal mortality. Thus, spacing and having fewer children was a program priority for the Bangladesh government and USAID's assistance. I was glad to be in a position and working on the program that provided options to the women for the betterment of their health and that of their children.

During the year as a PSC in the Bangladesh USAID Mission, I worked with a wonderful and highly professional health office staff. In a predominately Muslim country, it was challenging to convince families to have fewer children, even when survey after survey showed that women wanted fewer children than the average of six or seven. Plus, high maternal mortality rates also indicated the need for improved maternal health services in the clinics and getting women to accept the services, especially family planning and spacing their child births. It was a tough sell, especially in the rural areas. We needed women from the villages and neighborhood to do the outreach work, but we knew having women working for money outside the house, especially in a traditional Muslim society and for family planning, was going to be difficult. We knew they would be taking risks. However, once some of the women brought their paychecks home, resistance from their husbands and mothers-in-laws softened and their status in the household improved. Follow-up research also showed that when woman earned money, they were more likely to spend it on their kid's health and food. By the end of my contract, we had recruited hundreds of women as field health workers.

The family planning program in Bangladesh was a success. Fertility rates started to drop as did child and maternal deaths. I felt proud to be part of the program helping women and children. The program saved the lives of many women and children who would have otherwise died in unwanted child births and kids from malnutrition.

In 1987, working and travelling in Bangladesh was not easy. On field trips, my colleagues and I often stayed in hotels and guest houses with limited amenities, such as water, especially hot water. On one of my first trips to Chittagong, after returning from a long day in the field visiting clinics and speaking with women and children, I wanted nothing more than a hot shower. I went to the bathroom and saw a bucket under the tap, one tap with one knob, so only cold water and that was okay with me. There were no towels. I went to the reception and asked for some towels. Fifteen minutes later, a young man knocked on the door and I saw he had a pile of towels folded in his arms that he thrust toward me. I took them thanking him and then realized they were all wet. He said the sun had not been out for days as it had been raining so he could not dry them. That was a good lesson for me to be better prepared next time.

Some of the health centers and villages were not accessible by road, even if they were not very far away. We could only access such places part of the way by road and then would have to take ferries, adding more time away from home. For me, it was all good as I liked my job and believed that I was helping. I enjoyed my ferry trips and seeing the countryside. I was happier being with the women and children I was there to help than in the office.

All of us worked long days, but it did not seem to matter. I saw then that people bond differently in hardship workplaces. One of the staff from the US started an annual rickshaw race, another organized an annual mango-rama food competition where all dishes had to be made from mangoes. We played catch in our backyards with our colleagues on weekends. We were like one big family that depended on each other for emotional support and entertainment. I remember during one of the worst floods in Dhaka all the streets were knee deep in water making it difficult to get out of the house. A friend who had a rubber raft and I would transport water and other supplies to different houses. Political *hartals* (strikes and shutdowns) by one party or the other were frequent occurrences and hard to get used to. At times these *hartals* lasted for days. For security reasons we were asked to stay in our houses. Without cable and few English channels on the local TV station, passing time during the *hartals* was nerve wracking.

Living and working in Bangladesh was emotionally hard for me. I was used to poverty growing up in India, but nothing like what I had witnessed in Bangladesh, especially after heavy rains and flooding. News of families dying in the floods and homes destroyed year after year was hard to accept. Scenes of people placing babies and or kids in baskets and floating them away from their water-filled homes, hoping that someone would rescue them, were heart breaking. Worst was seeing corpses on the side of the road with a family member sitting next to them begging for money to perform burial rights.

The PSC job was a two-year contract job. As a contractor, I would need to look for jobs every couple of years when my contract ended. USAID was not hiring full-time employees. The Reagan administration had imposed a hiring freeze and a reduction in force. Once again, my friend Mike Jordan in Washington, DC, informed me that the agency had a special waiver to hire health officers. There was an extreme shortage of health staff, especially in Africa. Congress had tripled US assistance to Africa to prevent the spread of HIV/AIDS and USAID needed health officers to help manage the programs. I applied and passed the written exam, the interview, and was officially hired as a foreign service officer with USAID. I was almost fifty, the age at which USAID employees could retire, and I was finally starting my career. I owe Mike for being there for me and for helping me get established in my career path.

Burkina Faso

My first post as a foreign service officer and a diplomat was to Burkina Faso in West Africa. I had to learn French as it was the working language in Burkina Faso, once a French colony. For the next several months, I was in Washington, DC, learning French at the Foreign Services Institute (FSI). I moved to Ouagadougou, the capital of Burkina Faso in 1991. I knew little about Burkina Faso or about West Africa in general. As director of the health office, I was responsible for the largest health budget in the region due to the HIV/AIDS pandemic. In addition, my office provided technical support to the ministry of health for maternal childcare and nutrition programs.

Emotionally it was a hard assignment as we were losing our staff, along with many more in the country, to HIV/AIDS. I remember how helpless and sad I felt while sitting next to my HIV/AIDS coordinator and senior Burkinabe staff member as he lay dying on a bed in the special wing of the local hospital. He was responsible for managing the HIV/AIDS assistance programs. He advised the government on policies to introduce and implement HIV/AIDS prevention programs in the country, yet here he was in the hospital dying of the disease. He knew what the risks were. Yet, he did not practice what he was advising. His three wives were also diagnosed with HIV/AIDS. I learned later that he had married his third wife when he knew he had AIDS. I was angry with him, but he was dying. I realized as I did twenty years earlier, during my social work field assignment in the Delhi slums, that introducing new technologies and changing deep-rooted cultural beliefs and behavior is difficult and it takes time.

In the early days of the pandemic when someone died, people did not want to acknowledge it was because of AIDS. "He died of pneumonia," the relatives would say. Even the official records did not log the cause of death as HIV/AIDS. But that changed over time as the pandemic could no longer be ignored. The government and people of Burkina Faso did accept that the epidemic was real, but it took much longer than I had hoped for, and many lives were lost before preventive methods were accepted even when available. It was heartbreaking to go to funerals every other day.

During my tour in Burkina Faso, I saw that the use of condoms had increased, which was then the only means, other than abstinence, to prevent the spread of AIDS and subsequent death; there were no antiretroviral drugs available. USAID was the main agency assisting the ministry of health in providing condoms and educating people on safe sex. By the time I left the assignment, there was a better understanding of how HIV/AIDs spread and the means to prevent it or minimize its risk, and hospital records were showing a decline in deaths due to HIV/AIDS. I wondered how much longer it would have taken and how many more lives would have been lost without US assistance.

Another successful USAID project was the Famine Early Warning System (FEWS) implemented by a contractor. I was impressed by how the information about weather patterns, and food production helped donor agencies make informed decisions about food shortages in advance and plan for it. The data helped farmers adjust their planting and harvesting schedules.

Unfortunately, in 1994, for budgetary reasons, Washington decided to close smaller US-AID missions in the region. At the request of the ambassador, I was appointed the acting USAID director to stay on and oversee the closing. Shutting programs properly with minimum impact on the lives of our staff and the recipients of our programs, was a priority for me and our ambassador. The US staff was reassigned to other posts. Terminating contracts of the Burkinabe staff who had served USAID for years was the hardest part of the process. In a poor country such as Burkina Faso, a single earning family member often provided for many not only in his and her family but for their extended families in their villages.

When we closed the doors, all contracts had been terminated with enough time to phase down programs and to transfer ongoing approved programs to the regional office in Abidjan. We had enough time to work with donors to commit to more assistance for programs such as HIV/AIDS. We had time to transfer financial responsibility to the regional mission and appropriately dispose of all equipment and vehicles. And most importantly, with the help of the ambassador, we found employment for our Burkina staff. It took two years, but in the end as hard as it was, I felt good that we did it the right way.

Burkina Faso had special significance for me. It was my first job representing the United States. At the beginning, I was too formal and too official and afraid that I would make some terrible diplomatic blunder. I was overly cautious in meetings. My ambassador was helpful in mentoring me as I was a first tour officer. Over time, as I relaxed, I discovered that I was good at balancing the right amount of business with informal conversations to develop trusting relationships with my counterparts. I also realized that I was not afraid to make hard decisions when needed.

Burkina Faso was also the place where Jeffrey entered my life. I met him at my welcome party, the first day of my arrival in Ouagadougou. After playing squash and tennis for over a year, we started seeing each other seriously. Two weeks before I left Burkina Faso in September 1995, Jeffrey and I got married. Our wedding reception which in a way was my farewell to Burkina Faso, was hosted at the U.S Ambassador's residence. Dancing until late at night to the beat of the Burkina drummers who were young Burkinabe friends I played tennis with, was one of the best going away parties of my career.

In the US Foreign Service, we move every couple of years. In hardship countries, our tours often are for two years, but we can extend during the annual bidding cycle that announces all vacant positions for the coming year. In countries with better living conditions, our tours can be for two tours, meaning four years. My Burkina Faso tour was for two years, but I had extended for another tour to help with the close out. Thus, when the bid list came out in 1994, I put my preference for the general development officer position in Almaty. The regional USAID mission was responsible to fund and manage reforms in the Central Asian countries of the former Soviet Union, including Uzbekistan, Kyrgyzstan, Turkmenistan, Kazakhstan, and Tajikistan. The office I would be assigned to would have a broader set of programs to manage, which I thought would be a step forward in my career.

Central Asia

USAID started working in the Central Asia Republics soon after their independence in 1992. I was amongst the second group of US staff to be posted there and knew very little about the region. To me it was all part of one country, the Soviet Union. Transitioning the countries from centrally controlled economies to market-based systems through privatizations was the goal for the US assistance. USAID was the primary agency to implement the large congressionally approved funds for the region. I was excited to be part of what I believed was one of a lifetime experience and an experiment in change. USAID Regional Mission in Almaty was responsible for managing all assistance, with small offices in each of the countries for coordination purposes.

My office was called the Social Transition Office with oversight responsibilities for reforming the health sector, developing the non-government sector, privatizing the pension system, advancing the role of civil society, and supporting and creating an independent media. I was the deputy director of the office and directly responsible for the regional health reform project.

I had been told to pack minimum household effects as all American staff would be living in apartments as then there were very few houses available for renting. I was also told to bring an adequate supply of my favorite foods and toiletries as there was not much available in the stores. Toilet paper and detergent were high on the list. I knew I would have to learn Russian as it was the official working language then. Thus, for the first three months after arrival, I had one-on-one Russian lessons in my apartment.

I travelled constantly to all the countries in Central Asia. We were introducing new concepts and reforms, thus being on the ground to meet people and to discuss the new methodologies required us American staff in USAID to travel quite a bit. It was not easy to get to many countries such as Turkmenistan and Tajikistan where flights were limited. I often spent long hours at Tashkent airport making the connection to Turkmenistan. In 1995, most flights from Almaty to Tajikistan and Turkmenistan were through Uzbekistan. Road travel, except to Bishkek, was not possible due to the distance, poor infrastructure and the time it would take going by road. In the early stages of the reforms, there were more frequent trips as we had to negotiate all aspects of the programs with the host country technical ministries and ministries of economy, finance, and foreign affairs. Much of what we were introducing or offering was new, but countries had bought into the reform process, at least outwardly.

We, donors and host counterparts were learning as we implemented reforms. There were no examples and guidelines from other countries. The process of reforming and restructuring at the scale and across sectors was enormous and new to all of us. Much has been documented since then by experts about what was done right or wrong, but for me, it was an exhilarating experience to be part of such a major change process. In my interactions with the host government colleagues, I found them to be extremely interested in the reform process, but the willingness and commitment to change at the speed we expected varied from country to country.

I absolutely loved my time in Central Asia, both professionally and personally. As hard as the travel and reform process was, I was a bit giddy with the thought that we were making fundamental changes for the betterment of the people. There was energy in our mission. No one complained about long hours and travelling difficulties. We all accepted it as part of the challenge. We saw change happening right in front of our eyes. More government-held entities were privatizing. We saw grocery stores which previously had minimum items and long lines, getting busier and filling with a broader range of goods. We saw restaurants opening, and we would get excited at the new pizza place to go to after work.

We could buy toilet paper and detergent. There was cheese in the stores. Young women and men were hired by new grocery stores to help customers. New businesses were opening. New buildings and houses were being constructed. Health clinics were better equipped. The health sector was introducing new concepts such as family doctors and introducing preventive and primary health care services. We saw more US businesses operating in the region. Some of us in the field could see how the reforms were benefiting those in influential positions. Some of us were concerned with the oligarchs taking advantage of privatization, but we hoped that over time things would balance out as progress was made in rule of law and governance.

As one colleague said, "The overall policy agenda that we support to transfer ownership from the public to the private sector will make it impossible for communism to return." That meant putting the legal framework in place along with the commercial laws and judicial reforms to interpret them. We were idealistic. I was a bit naïve to think that so much could be changed in such a short time. I did not quite understand the strong hold of the old system, still prevalent, in the echelons of decision making.

Sadly, for many, especially in the rural areas, without the safety net of the old system, life became more difficult as the gulf between rich and poor widened. I was told by many that the reforms were not benefiting all equally and there were many more homeless people on the streets. Overtime, the reforms benefited those already in power, setting the stage for the oligarchs to accumulate more power and wealth. During my tour, I noticed more and more homeless people begging on the streets. On field trips, I could see that rural areas lagged and that the benefits of the reforms in the capital and in other urban areas were not trickling as I had hoped.

I accompanied our ambassadors in each country to many meetings to discuss important reform measures. USAID had technical and financial resources but needed the leverage from the ambassador's office to demonstrate that what USAID did was important to US foreign policy goals.

The US government was the lead donor in the 90s and other international organizations, such as the World Bank, sought to partner with the US because we had the leverage. I saw the benefits of working together as one US team. The ambassador, our embassy staff, and USAID presented a unified approach, without which we could not have accomplished as much as we did in the time frame. Over time, each government in the region chose its own course and path to economic growth and democracy. The US assistance, in my opinion, opened the door to change in the region and set the groundwork for the countries to follow their own economic and democratic paths.

On a personal level, there were challenges. The vodka drinking was a mandatory ritual at that time at all events no matter what time of day. For me, this required some navigating by trying to excuse myself with "that is enough—I have asthma and have to be careful." My hosts would say, "Americans don't know that vodka is good for asthma," as they filled my glass with another shot. Not being able to speak freely even in your own apartment was another as we feared there were surveillance systems installed in our apartments. I remember returning home from work one day and noticed muddy footprints on the floor and my bathtub full of water. I knew that my housekeeper could not have left the water in the tub or had someone with large feet leave foot fronts on my floor. I knew I had had a visitor in my absence.

During those early days of transition, making friends was hard. Propaganda against the US was still fresh in everybody's mind and Americans were bad people and thus my neighbors did not trust me or even look at me when passing each other in the staircase. It took more than a year for my neighbor to greet me. One day when she found out that I was originally from India, she hesitantly asked me if I knew Raj Kapoor, a popular Indian movie star. Indian movies were frequently shown in the theaters in the region. Finding an opening, I lied and said "yes." I wanted her to talk to me more and we had a few short conversations after that, mostly in the hallway. She knew no English and even after a year of study, my Russian was poor, but I was happy that we both tried to converse a bit and be neighborly. However, I was never invited to her apartment, and she never accepted my invitation to visit me in mine.

Through my Russian teacher I did get some insight into how life had been before. Sometimes after lessons, Tatiana, my Russian teacher would talk to me in English. When I asked her how life was then and now, she said that at the start, the people were enthusiastic about reforms, but as time passed, it became clear that the reforms were not helping all equally. She said that everybody got the opportunity to buy and own their apartments at very low cost, but then the influential people offered to buy property that seemed desirable to many. Over time, many who sold their apartments were rendered homeless.

She said, "It's good that we don't have to worry about someone saying something or fabricating something and being imprisoned or sent to the gulags. People don't have to live in fear." But then she added, "But we are living in uncertainty because we don't know what to expect, what not to expect. Everybody's on their own and we've lost the safety net. There is no safety net if we do not have a job."

She thought for a moment and said, "Before you had a house, many were assigned a *dacha* (a summer place and land where they could grow vegetables and fruits). After some years of government work, we knew when we would get a car, and an apartment, and when we would get a *dacha*. Everything was planned and organized for us. But now everyone is on their own."

The new opening of the Central Asia Region made it an attractive region for my family and friends to visit, especially my family. My mother visited in 1996. We flew to Kiev and drove to Samarkand and Tashkent. It was the highlight of my stay in Central Asia from a tourist point of view. She had read about Timur and the Mogul rulers that conquered India came from that region before the Soviet Union. She knew more than I did about the region, especially Uzbekistan. It was one of the places on her bucket list that she had thought she would never be able to visit. I was so happy to make her wish come true. My brother and his wife came a year later and did the same route and then my mother returned with my two nieces in 1998 again. She loved the region. She felt that her ancestors had come from there, and maybe they did.

Armenia and Nagorno Karabakh

My tour in Central Asia was coming to an end, the deputy mission director, a senior management position in Armenia was on the bid list. The Central Asia deputy mission director who was assigned to Armenia as mission director encouraged me to bid on the deputy position. We worked closely in Central Asia, and she was familiar with my style of working. Central Asia was my second tour with USAID, and Washington head office thought that I was too new to the agency to take on a senior management position. She convinced them that I was the right person. I moved to Armenia in September 1999.

Armenia then was not the easiest place to live. After the Spitak earthquake, the nuclear power plant was shut down, leading to an energy crisis. Not until 1995, when the second unit of the plant was operational, did the cold and dark years of life in the country end. People would still talk about living in darkness and having to eat by candlelight, of burning their furniture for heat from the fire. The country was in recovery, but infrastructure was still lacking.

USAID office was walking distance to my

house. My walk home passed the parliamentary building and then followed a shortcut through a neighborhood where along grapevine-lined cobblestone streets, I would see women sitting outside their apartments chatting and kids playing. Once they were familiar with me seeing me walking by almost every evening, they were willing to talk. I started to stop and say a few words of greeting or asking about their kids. I wanted them to know me as their neighbor.

One day not long after I arrived in Yerevan, I was wrapping up work, anticipating my walk when I heard alarms go off. I was told we were in lockdown mode. It was some time before we got the news that there had been a shooting in the parliamentary building as a session was about to start. Armed men entered and shot the reform-minded prime minister, and two other parliamentarians who had recently won the elections on a reform agenda. It was not until late that night that we were able to leave. A couple of weeks later, I was in the parliament house for a meeting and saw bloodstains on the walls. The assassination was a stark reminder for me of the consequences and risks of political reform.

In Burkina Faso, I had learned how to close a mission and how emotionally hard that was. In Armenia, my experience was more positive. In 1998, the Armenia USAID mission had become a standalone mission. Previously it was supported by many services provided by the USAID/Georgia mission in Tbilisi. As the first deputy in the post, I was responsible for establishing internal management and control systems. It was rewarding to see a mission and staff grow as an independent entity and function as teams without having to rely on the regional mission for approvals. The USAID/Armenia mission provided support to the health sector, the private sector, including energy, and support to democratic institutions and the social sector.

USAID/Armenia also had a separate congressionally approved budget for assistance programs in the enclave of Nagorno-Karabakh (NK). Due to the political sensitivities related to NK's status as a disputed territory, the US presence was limited to having one senior US foreign service officer to visit the enclave for project monitoring. The mission director assigned that role to me, and I became the main contact point for our programs in Nagorno-Karabakh. We supported a housing and school rehabilitation program, water reconstruction, and a women-owned small business initiative. Clearing deadly landmines and other leftover military ordinances was a high priority implemented by HALO. Landmines had been laid in NK since the early 1990s when the war between Azerbaijan and Armenia began. It was estimated that much of the agricultural and nonagricultural land was covered in mines, leading to the death of many innocent civilians. With our assistance program, much of the land was eventually cleared of mines and families could return and start farming again. Children could go back to school in the newly reconstructed school buildings. But clearing mines was never-ending work, with every new skirmish, there would be new mines to clear.

I would visit NK once every three months with an Armenia staff member. It took about three hours on a brand-new two-lane highway built by diaspora funds to reach Stepanakert, the capital of NK. There were times when I would be meeting with a farming family and a land mine would go off close to us. By the end of my tour, I had covered most of the territory of NK. I could meet with the recipients and implementing partners, but I could not meet with any officials since the enclave was not officially recognized by the US as an independent country. As the main contact person for NK, I would often be involved in senior level meetings at the embassy and with Washington staff regarding the peace negotiations.

I would also accompany and help coordinate congressional delegations to NK. Most of the congressional visits included meeting with the displaced population and visits to the villages destroyed by the different military skirmishes, which continued off and on between Azerbaijan and Armenia armies. There were times when I was hopeful of a resolution. When I talked to the people, they would say that this is our home, our ancestors lived here. But I didn't get the feeling that they were hopeful. Marie Yovanovitch's book *Lessons from the Edge* covers this subject well.

I was also the point person to work with the Armenia diaspora living in the U.S who actively lobbied for congressional funding for Armenia. Working with the many different Armenian diaspora groups, passionate and well-meaning people who wanted to help their people and homeland, was often challenging. Each group had its own priorities and preferences as to what programs should be funded in Armenia. They had political support due to their influence in the US Congress. It was often hard to explain to them that USAID was bound by contractual and financial policies and guidelines, and that we could not just sign a check over to them. Through negotiating and collaborating with them, I learned how to balance our varying interests and policy priorities with those of the diaspora. The women's health center for breast cancer screening was one area we partnered with one of the diaspora organizations. At that time, there were no services available for early detection and treatment of breast cancer in Armenia, and USAID resources were not adequate to cover the full range of needs. Thus, partnering with the diaspora organization, we were able bring much needed services to many women who would have otherwise had to go overseas for treatment or die.

In 2001, I extended my tour in Armenia for two years in the hopes of moving into the director's position. The director had completed her tour, but Washington had another candidate in mind. I was disappointed. I knew the country and the programs and had developed a rapport with our counterparts, but I lacked an advocate amongst the senior USAID staff in Washington. I did not want to stay in Armenia doing the same work I had been doing for the previous two years, so I started to look for other mission director positions.

Eritrea

One evening, I got a call from the ambassador I had worked with in Burkina Faso. He had been assigned as the ambassador to Eritrea and wanted to know if I would be interested in heading the USAID programs in Eritrea. Finalizing assignment details and transferring mid tour took some time, but finally my assignment to Eritrea was approved. I went directly from Armenia to Eritrea in 2001. For every new assignment, Mission Directors are officially sworn in, often in Washington, DC. I opted to be sworn in by the US Ambassador at post so that all the staff I would be managing could attend. I used the Constitution for my oath. My spouse, Jeffrey, held the Constitution on which I placed my left hand while I raised my right hand and repeated after the ambassador:

"I, Jatinder Cheema do solemnly swear that I will support and defend the constitution of the United States against all enemies, foreign and domestic; that I will bear true faith and allegiance to the same; that I take this obligation freely, without any mental reservations or purpose of evasion; and that I will well and faithfully discharge the duties of the office on which I am about to enter. So, help me God."

Taking this oath was a transforming experience for me. While repeating the words of the oath after my ambassador, I felt a deep sense of personal and professional responsibility to my country.

Before going to the post, I was briefed about the difficulties involved in implementing and managing development under the strained bilateral relations and an authoritarian Eritrean president. I was told that a few of my predecessors had been declared persona non grata (PNG) and had to leave the country. In diplomatic situations, when the host country declares that a diplomatic staff is unwelcome, it is a prelude to expelling them from the country. Even knowing this, I thought how difficult could it be? I knew that many of the senior staff of Eritrean ministries and organizations had been educated in the West, many at US universities. So, they must share the same values as us about rule of law and good governance, I thought. I did not realize until I got to post, the level of control the president of Eritrea had when it came to international agencies and relations, especially those involving the US.

Humanitarian assistance was USAIDs largest program in Eritrea. Thirty years of conflict between Eritrea and Ethiopia had left many people in need of food aid. Similarly, the health services were short of supplies and medicines. Our health assistance program was filling a much-needed gap along with other donor agencies. Although the programs were much needed, the government did not trust foreign agencies, especially US organizations, and made it difficult for our implementing partners to operate. In Eritrea, I learned how important it was to work with other donors, bilateral and multilateral and have the support of my ambassador. The Eritrean ruler made it difficult for donors to implement programs, thus there was a need for a unified approach. I initiated a bi-weekly donors meeting to discuss problems we all faced and how to address those through political *demarches*.

One of my challenges in Eritrea was to get a memorandum of understanding signed with the government to make the work of our implementing agencies easier and provide some safeguards. In the health sector, I was able to develop a working relationship with the minister of health, who understood the need for health assistance in the rural areas. But I had no counterpart minister for our humanitarian and food aid work. I had to work with the senior advisor to the Eritrean president regarding donor coordination and assistance to negotiate the memorandum of understanding for our humanitarian assistance. Due to our strained bilateral relations, and the government becoming more suspicious of all donors, especially the US, we needed some agreement to establish policies and tax status of US non-government organizations to streamline delivery of humanitarian assistance and to ensure their safety in the country.

After several meetings going over the draft memorandum of understanding, I thought I had convinced him of the need for such a document. We were close to signing it. But then, something changed. A month passed, and his office would not schedule a meeting with me to finalize the date for the official signing. His office said that he was not available when my secretary tried to make an appointment. We knew that he was in town and was holding meetings with the Italians and the French and other agencies. So, one day, I showed up in his office and announced to his secretary that I was there to see him. I was told he was busy. I said fine and found a seat just outside his office in the waiting room and took out a book of Anton Chekhov's short stories. I always had a book in my bag and short stories worked well when I had to wait for meetings. Several times his secretary told me that he was booked for the day. I told her that I had time and would wait. Finally, around 6:00 p.m., he emerged from his office. Since I was a US diplomat, he could not openly ignore me. He said, "why are you waiting?" He turned to his secretary, reprimanding her for not letting him know that I was waiting. I smiled inwardly. I knew he knew I was there. We finally met and once again I made the case why an agreement such as this would be good for his country's people. I did get a final date from him for the official signing of the document. Patience, that I had learned when working in the slums of Delhi, worked here.

Another challenge for the US staff was to protect our Eritrean staff. We knew that they were under pressure to report on what discussions took place inside our embassy and USAID offices. We needed to be careful with what we said and what we required of our Eritrean staff to ensure that we did not put them in a compromising situation.

Traveling for work and for tourism was possible when I first got to Eritrea. Eritrea has a mix of landscape. The central plateau, where Asmara is located, is a foundation of crystalline rock. I am not a geologist, but the evening light around Asmara is so deep with many shades and hues of red, orange and yellow that I became an amateur photographer during my stay there. It became my routine on weekends and after work to take my camera and wander the streets and neighborhoods of Asmara to take pictures. Massawa, on the Red Sea and part of the coastal area has semi desert, unspoiled beaches and divine snorkeling and scuba diving. Plus, the Italian art deco architecture of Asmara and the very different Arabic architecture of the coastal cities, made Eritrea a unique place for tourism. For many of us, going to the Red Sea was a nice get away from the work environment. My mother and my family visited me as did my best friend Karen.

Over time, the government put more and more restrictions on travel, and we had to get special permission to leave the capital, which often took days, making monitoring of projects difficult. The government's restrictions caused some personal hardships for me as a family. Jeffrey was working in Ethiopia with the World Food Program. He would visit me every three months on a small UN airplane that flew between Ethiopia and Eritrea for UN operations. However, the Eritrean government blocked his entry one time. He had a U.S diplomatic passport and a multiple entry visa to Eritrea. When I got a call from him that he was at the airport and was denied entry, I reached out to our ambassador who intervened by personally going to the airport and demanding to see the Eritrean counterpart at the Ministry of Foreign Affairs. After hours of waiting Jeffrey was allowed to enter the country. No one explained the reason, but we all knew that the government was making life difficult for American diplomats.

My job at USAID was nonpolitical, however, I was often called upon to be the "Chargé d'affaris" (acting ambassador) when our ambassador was out of the country or in between ambassadors. In that role, I performed the functions of the ambassador and had to deal with our bilateral issues with the government of Eritrea often meeting with the President and staff from the foreign ministries and the military when we had delegations from Washington. Having this broader exposure helped me better understand the context within which I was managing the assistance program.

Our US staff, all frustrated by the working environment, turned to each other for support and became like one big family. The American Club with its tennis court became a hub for social interactions. At the start of my tour, some of the Eritrean counterparts would come to play with us and we would be invited to the local tennis club, but over time these interactions became limited, and I felt more and more isolated from the people I was supposed to work with in the Eritrean government and from the Eritrean people, I was there to help.

Despite the challenges, I did complete my tour as the USAID Director in Eritrea and was not declared persona non grata (PNG). It became somewhat of a joke between my boss in Washington and me. Whenever we spoke on the phone, he would first ask, "Are you PNG yet?"

I would say, "Maybe soon."

My efforts and success in making some advancements in our humanitarian and health programs despite the political environment were recognized by my superiors. My ambassador, when submitting my evaluation, mentioned that I was not afraid of taking risks when it benefited our policy. I suppose all of it paid off and I was promoted to the rank of a senior foreign service officer, which is the highest grade in the US foreign service.

West Africa

In 2005, after nearly four years in Eritrea, I knew it was time to leave. I was interested in Afghanistan at that point. The country held a special significance for me. My grandfather was posted in Peshawar as the income tax officer for the British prior to the India independence and would tell stories about his travels to Afghanistan, which was also under his jurisdiction. In 1971, when I was living in Pakistan for a short period with my ex-husband, I had traveled by road from Islamabad to Kabul through the Kyber pass. I imagined Alexander marching through the Kyber pass and wondered how those massive armies passed through the narrow gorge. I spent two days in Kabul and the scenes of colorful markets full of carpets and food stalls grilling lamb made me want to know more about the country.

I believed, then, in all the reasons why the US was in Afghanistan. I wanted to be part of the relief our development programs would bring to the women and children and the people and help change the systems destroyed by the Taliban oppression. I wanted to experience firsthand how our Diplomacy, Defense and Development work together. However, the timing was not right in that no senior level positions were open in the USAID/Afghanistan Mission when I had to move from Eritrea. The Africa/Bureau management recommended me for heading the West Africa Regional Programs (WARP) office, based in Accra/Ghana.

WARP was responsible only for technical support for projects in health, agriculture, trade and education primarily in West African countries under the provisions of a regional budget. Other non-technical support was provided by the bilateral missions where there were contracting, financial, legal and administrative staff. This separation of services from different locations made coordination complicated and some ambassadors unhappy. Finally, a decision was made in Washington to expand the role of WARP and make it an independent USAID/West Africa Regional Mission and consolidate all technical and non-technical support and staff under one mission. This decision happened soon after I arrived at my post in 2005. I was thus the first Mission Director for USAID/West Africa and was assigned to lead the reorganization effort in coordination with other mission directors in the region.

At times, I felt that the task of reorganizing was too much, but we got it done. In one year, we had the West Africa Regional Mission operational. I can't say enough about the hard work and professionalism of the staff who were drafting documents, calculating budget needs, amending and ensuring timely approvals from all involved, and smoothing the transfer of staff. Without their commitment and the long hours that they put into this exercise, I am not sure we would have completed the task in a year. The mandate for the regional mission was to manage and support programs in countries where there was no USAID presence and develop and manage regional programs, such as trade initiatives, communicable diseases and agriculture.

Working at a regional level can be challenging. The constant travel by many of the technical and support staff, coordinating programs across many countries, some facing insurgencies from Islamic groups, or ethnic conflicts, was physically taxing. Sometimes there were travel restrictions and sometimes it was hard to find counterparts willing to work and travel in conflict areas.

Despite the difficulties, our regional programs in agriculture, health, and trade promotion were successful. Our trade hubs increased the trade of goods in the region, providing opportunities for many small businesses to flourish. It created space for US goods to enter the market as systems were established, and laws were put in place to facilitate trade. We introduced new technologies so farmers could better track prices and when and where to sell their grain. Our assistance in HIV/AIDS prevention was crucial, especially targeting transport routes where so much of the population flow between countries took place. Programs in media, democracy, and rule of law were less favorable to a regional platform as each country was at a different point of development with their democratic processes.

I had to also accommodate politically mandated initiatives. I remember a difficult trip to Equatorial Guinea (EG) where I travelled with my legal officer to negotiate a memorandum of understanding between the USG and EG. I knew nothing about EG except what I read in the book called Tropical Gangsters. Because of its oil, the US had business interests in the country and thus we needed a partnership agreement. I was not sure that the host country had completely bought into the agreement, making me and our lawyer go to one city after the other chasing our main point of contact with the government to discuss the details of the agreement. We finally got the draft prepared to send it to Washington. I had left the region before it was implemented, but it was a learning experience for me to balance my role as a development advisor and implement our foreign policy interests, outside of development.

At the start of my tour, I was nervous working with so many counterparts in so many countries and with so many ambassadors. I soon learned how amazing and understanding people can be when working in difficult environments. Many countries in the region were in one kind of crisis or another, caused by internal or external influences. Countries such as Burkina Faso, Mali, Niger that appeared to be at a breaking point in political and economic spheres in 1991 when I was first posted in the region, were being affected by the Islamic jihadist movement as well as internal insurgencies. Given the changing nature of our environment, USAID received special funding for anti-terrorism, an area new to those of us in development. We worked with our embassies and our defense forces in the region to develop and implement new community-based programs to counter terrorism. We were all trying to do our best in an extremely volatile environment. Sometimes I did get complaints from ambassadors, but everyone understood and realized that we were working in challenging environments.

In 2008, I was nearing the age of 65, the mandatory age at that time for retirement in the US Foreign Service, and on that birthday, July 27, 2008, I officially retired.

USAID Coda

I had no idea what I was going to do next—or where I was going to live. I had left the US in 1985 and had not been back to live since. I would go home on leave to see my sister and friends and Jeffrey's family, but we had never discussed where we would live after I retired. I had a house in the Washington, DC, metropolitan area, and Jeffrey's family lived in Wisconsin. My sister lived in Berkeley, California, but there was no way we could afford to buy a house and live in Berkeley on our pensions and social security. Jeffrey had a cabin in Wisconsin, so we bought a condo on Williamson Street in Madison. I was not ready to quit working yet.

I knew that USAID was short of senior officers due to the staff reduction and a hiring freeze in the 1990s, which had left a vacuum at senior management levels. I let senior management know that I was available to work. The Africa Bureau offered me a position in Liberia. The mission director there had to leave early and or had retired. However, unbeknown to me, at the time, someone had complained to a senior manager in the administrator's office about my management style. I never learned what the exact complaint was and who had complained, but my posting was stalled. No one would tell me why. I knew I had a solid professional reputation. I was frustrated and hurt as this is not how I wanted to end my career, that I thought was successful.

I did not know how to correct this misunderstanding, who to see and where the decision was held up. The head of human resources was not helpful. All he said was that the message was coming from above, and that I should hand in my badge and clear out my office, without looking at me while he kept working on his computer. I had expected more from the head of human resources, who I knew and thought of as a colleague and a friend. It was a rude awaking to see that side of our bureaucracy that abide by "decision from above" without questioning.

I did not want to end my career on a doubt. I wanted to know the truth and set the record straight. A friend in the Africa Bureau suggested that I request a meeting with the USAID Counselor in the USAID Administrator's office. During the meeting I learned that someone, who personally knew the acting USAID administrator, and had worked for me in the USAID/West Africa mission, had complained that I was a screamer and a racist. My first reaction was to laugh. I could not believe that after all these years and having much positive feedback from my subordinates, supervisors and ambassadors, not to mention all the Superior and Meritorious awards I had received, that this one person's comment, without verification, had put a question mark on my career. I was angry and when I am angry my first reaction is to cry—I have been like this for years and dislike that side of me as it shows me in a weak position. But this time my tears were of pain, hurt and unfairness of it all. Finally, after I provided my perspective about the context and some performance background about the person who I thought might have complained, the issue was resolved. I requested the counselor to follow up for verification and feedback from other staff in the mission who had worked with me and all the ambassadors in the region, but I was told that would not be necessary. My assignment was approved.

The Liberia position was filled by then. The Africa Bureau offered another post, as there were vacancies in number of countries, but I had accepted an offer to go to Afghanistan by then.

Afghanistan

The opportunity to go to Afghanistan happened by chance. One evening I was having a drink with a colleague, who was a senior manager and responsible for staffing the Afghanistan USAID mission. I was venting about what had happened to me and how hurt I was. He knew of my work in other Missions and turned around and asked, "you want to go to Afghanistan?" Apparently, he had been trying to fill one of the two senior positions in the mission. He did not know that I was available until that moment as he had heard that I was going to Liberia. I jumped at the idea. I had been wanting to go to Afghanistan since 2005. Afghanistan was a non-family post and Jeffrey stayed in Madison.

My mother was not pleased with my decision. She kept herself up to date on the news and knew the dangers. When I told her that I would be living in a trailer, she could not understand why I wanted to do that. She said, "you have done enough good for the world, now retire and enjoy." It was hard for me to explain to her and my family and friends as to why I was doing this after retirement. I wanted to visit the places my grandfather had talked about, but more than that, I wanted to talk to the women and see for myself how much harm the Taliban had done, especially in case of girls' education and make it better. And I wanted the experience of working side-by-side with our military to see how development works in a war situation. I knew it would not be easy or safe.

As a senior staff, I was offered one of the few one-bedroom apartments, but I opted to live in a compound of trailers, or hooches, in military slang, where most of the USAID staff lived. The workday in the USAID compound in Kabul lacked a routine. Day and night were mixed up. At any given hour, I would find people in the office working, or in the gym, or sitting around the small space outside their hooches and talking to colleagues. My favorite exercise time was five in the morning, the only time when I found quietness. I would jog on the paved street constructed around the walled compound of rows of hooches, a gym, a canteen, the warehouse, the general services area, where the logistics team and cars were housed and a small shop like a convenience store where we could buy essentials. The compound was our little village.

I also got good at ducking under the bed every time there was a threat from a mortar attack, which was not that uncommon. I remember on two occasions, my vacation was postponed by a day or so because just as I was leaving for the airport, there was an emergency alert about an attack close to the Embassy. When I visited Madison on a rest and recuperation visit, I would jump at the slightest noise, because my body had trained itself to be in an alert mode.

I had many special moments during my tour in Kabul. For example, when I gave a talk to a class of women at the American University. They were studying for a certificate in computer sciences and software development. After my talk, I spent time with the young women to discuss what they would like to do after they finish. They all had career plans. At that moment, I forgot about the hardship of living and working in Afghanistan. I saw before me smiling and hopeful faces of these young women. To this day, I see those faces and can hear them telling me what they wanted to do in their lives. I am heartbroken to think what might have happened to them under the Taliban regime, once again.

Our field trips were limited due to security reasons but whenever I had the opportunity to talk to kids, farmers and other recipients, I felt hopeful despite all the difficulties we faced implementing programs in the conflict environment. I saw the limitations of doing development under war conditions and I wondered often if what we were doing would have a lasting impact. But at that time, I believed in our involvement in Afghanistan.

The highlight of my time living in the compound was the weekly visits to the market at the army base. The base had all the amenities, coffee shops and a restaurant, a bazaar to buy rugs and shopping, a place to get a massage and a haircut. I looked forward to those visits.

Then there was the Obama visited in 2008 when he was the democratic presidential nominee, the compound was abuzz with excitement. The sound of the black hawk descending on the compound helicopter pad made us all run to a small opening through the wall where we could see him enter the compound. I will never forget later at the inauguration reception at one of the hotels, that was cleared by security for the embassy to have the event, people crying with joy watching him on the large screen giving his speech.

On March 22, 2009, I left Kabul. I was invited for drinks and dinner three evenings in a row before my departure with colleagues with whom I had arrived in Kabul a year earlier. I had organized a cake and coffee party for the staff at the canteen the day before leaving. I thought I would be happy to be leaving. On the twenty first, all I had to do was pack my two suitcases and remove my pictures from the walls of the hootch. I reached out to take off the picture of my mother which was taped close to my pillow that I saw every evening I went to bed, then there were pictures of Jeffery and my other family members and my best friend Karen. Above the TV were David Hopper prints. On one wall were all the cards I had received during the year wishing me well or stay safe messages. My hootch had been my refuge. The pictures would comfort me. As I took them off and one by one and tore them, I felt I was dismantling my safe space. It was midnight when I finished cleaning up. I went for a walk around the compound—saying goodbye to the stray cats which had been adopted by different occupants. I did feel some relief when I passed the sandbags lining our hooches, knowing I would not have to see them again. I silently wished those left behind the best of health and to stay safe for the rest of their tour. I walked through my office and sat on my chair and reflected on whether I would do this again. I knew I would if the opportunity arose. There was still so much work to be done. Little did I know then what was to come.

Armenia Again

Leaving Afghanistan, I felt nothing else will compare to my work and life in Kabul. On the plane back, I wondered how easily I had accepted and become accustomed to a life with little choices. Before I had left Kabul, I was asked to return to Armenia. The director's position was vacant due to a medical evacuation. I agreed to go to Armenia. I was interested to see the changes that had taken place since I was there in 1999.

The Armenia of 2009 was quite different from the Armenia of 1999 concerning reforms and development. The private sector was stronger, there were no electricity shortages, and some safety nets such as the pension system, although not perfect, were in place. An active non-government sector was more involved in social and political issues. People had access to multiple media outlets. USAID programs were more mature and sustainable. Our relationship with our counterparts was more of a partnership where we agreed on common grounds and signed agreements to allocate funding for programs. The US foreign assistance budget was reduced over the years. I noticed that the Armenian diaspora had less involvement in influencing US assistance levels as compared to 1999. The Nagorno-Karabakh conflict was unresolved, but USAID had no special funding from congress to work in NK. The USAID mission and staff was well established, with many of the Armenian staff in leadership positions.

During my second tour, I was more comfortable in my role as the head of the mission than I was in 1999. The mission did not require hands-on work, as it did did when we first established the mission in 2009. All systems were in place and required normal monitoring and ensuring of efficiencies. There were personnel and mission morale and performance issues that required immediate attention, caused mainly by a gap in leadership at the USAID mission. I had the most supportive ambassador which helped make some difficult decisions. I sadly left Armenia in 2012 when USAID found a replacement to fill the position of the director. I returned to Madison.

On the plane to Madison from Washington, I was sitting next to a young man, who surprisingly enough was familiar with international development, USAID, and how US foreign assistance works. Previously, very few people in our Madison neighborhood knew much about what I did and about USAID. I was convinced he was a professor at the university. I learned later that he worked for the political arm of the non-profit advocacy group. He connected me with the volunteers working on the Obama campaign. I enrolled as a volunteer and as an election worker. I owe him for connecting me to the political activists in Madison. After the 2012 elections, I joined several neighborhood organizations and remained active in issues important to the community.

USAID short-term assignments

Between 2012 and 2017, I undertook short term assignments with USAID which included a year in Central Asia, three months in Sierre Leon and a month in Guinea Conakry.

The work in Sierre Leon was primarily to coordinate our Ebola efforts with CDC and other donors and to streamline coordination with the Guinea Conakry mission which provided oversight for the Sierre Leon office. I saw firsthand how US assistance was critical in managing the spread of Ebola in the region and making our own shores safer by establishing screening and monitoring systems. The month in Guinea Conakry was primarily to ensure that our end of the year funding was programmed. I had not been to Guinea Conakry before and was surprised at the poor infrastructure and lack of social services, such as garbage collection. I was not there long enough to know and understand the impact of our assistance program.

My year-long assignment to Central Asia 2016-2017 was hard. My mandate was to downsize the regional mission considering reduced regional budget over time and increased bilateral assistance budgets for other countries in the region, such Kyrgyzstan, Uzbekistan and Tajikistan. I agreed with the mandate. I was tasked to develop a reorganizational plan to reduce the Almaty office presence while right sizing staff in the countries where the assistance budget was increasing. It was a very difficult assignment. I tried to be fair to the staff by sharing as much as I could without causing unnecessary panic as I was not sure when the decision would be made to move forward with the reorganization. Although, I agreed with the reorganization as I felt downsizing was needed and some regional programs needed to close, I needed more political backing and firm decisions from the head office in Washington. I ended up making no one happy in the field. I also had to balance how much to share and when, often giving the impression that I was not being transparent. Given that decisions were not final, I did not want to cause unnecessary stress and affect staff morale in the mission. With the help of key staff, we did prepare a model for downsizing and reorganization, while providing oversight, start new projects, and guide and mentor our field staff.

No Regrets

Looking back, I feel content with my career and good about my achievements. At every post and in every position, I gave my best and learned from the mistakes that I made. Who would have thought when I was born in 1942 to a young Sikh family in Punjab, India, that one day I would be sitting across the table with the senior most US and host country officials and negotiating and discussing US policy and assistance programs? I look at myself in the mirror and I know my grandparents and parents would be proud of me.

Development is not perfect, but it plays an important part in implementing our foreign policy goals using soft power as development is often referred to. I feel so fortunate to have had a career where I could make a difference. In addition, I have had the opportunities to travel in so many countries and have so many wonderful experiences and adventures. Looking back, I have no regrets. In the process, I have learned important lessons.

I learned early in my career that, being a woman, I would need to navigate my career differently than if I was a man. I joined USAID at the same time as another male colleague who also was working in Bangladesh at the same time as I was, who had similar work experience as I did, and similar qualifications. He negotiated a better grade and salary at entry. I had made the same arguments as he had, regarding my experience and my qualifications. The response from a male human resources officer was that I should be grateful to have the opportunity, that it was the best they could do, and that getting in was important. I accepted that. My male colleague on the other hand did not have to hear that. He was offered what he had asked for. That stuck with me, and I decided then that if I were going to succeed and make it to the senior ranks, I would need to fight and advocate for myself and not sit back and accept what was handed to me.

My mother told me that I was precocious as a child, that I started reading early, talked like an adult, was inquisitive and learned fast, but I was also a quiet child. Growing up, I was comfortable being by myself if I had my books. I was comfortable doing my job, doing it well. Everyone would say that I was a hard worker. But I discovered that just hard work was not enough, I had to be at the table and needed to be heard. Thus, networking was a skill I had to learn. I was always comfortable with a small number of friends. This worked well for me until I started working and learned that I needed to be seen and heard and have a network of friends and colleagues who would have my back. Looking back at my career, I realized how important developing a network of friends was. I was always helped by someone I knew and who knew of my work. My advice to my colleagues, especially women, is to not depend on your work alone. Develop a network of a core group of people that you can rely on and trust to advocate for you. In my experience, women in USAID need this even more than men. It worked for me. Although I had a solid professional reputation, when it came to advancing my career, my core group looked out for me. They helped me make choices and advocated for me.

Working and living in less economically developed countries was a constant reminder of poverty surrounding me. Even in our government provided comfortable houses, every time I stepped in a shower with hot running water, often from a tank that was filled by our administrative services, I would think of those women and kids hauling water over their heads from long distances, in a bucket. That one bucket of water would likely be their only water for a few days. I would feel the unfairness of it all. Similarly, when

I found myself taking electricity for granted, in some cities provided by generators, I would think of the kids doing their homework by streetlights as they had no electricity at home. It was a consistent reminder to not take what I was doing and what I had for granted, and how much more we all had to do.

There were personal challenges. I remember a field trip to a village in Africa where it is common to sit in a circle on plastic mats, often on the ground under a tree, and drink out of a common bowl. The bowl, made of wood or a tree bark is often filled with local homemade brew. The bowl is passed around from person to person, each taking a sip. It is a gesture of hospitality and welcome to their community. The village head said a few welcoming words, and the bowl was passed around. Sitting in the circle, looking at the bowl, looking at each mouth it had touched and thinking, I must do this. I was never sure if I was being tested and what would happen if I passed the bowl without taking a sip. But I never did. I would take a deep breath and take a sip of the tart tasting drink, not sure what it was or where the water came from to make it and pass the bowl to the next person. I was often sick after each field trip when I was working in Africa.

There were situations where my personal preference and choice could have conflicted with the cultural and accepted practices in the country or community. In every situation, I tried to balance my actions in a way that hopefully would not offend my host. For example, drinking vodka. Drinking vodka was big during the 1990s. No matter what time of day or event. Luckily the culture had changed when I worked there again in 2012. During my first tour, I would try to find ways to discreetly empty my vodka shot behind a bush if I was outside, or I would find a seat next to someone I knew who could manage drinking better than me and would pour my vodka into their glass after they had emptied it. I found many ways to get rid of my vodka without offending my host. My excuse about asthma did not work, my leaving my glass full when another round was called for did not work as the host would insist and look offended. Another cultural practice that I had difficulty with was swallowing the goat eye. In Kazakhstan, it was customary for the host to give the grilled goat's eyeballs in a soup to the senior most guest of honor to mark the start of an event. I always made sure I had my supervisor with me when I knew that I would be offered the cup.

In Afghanistan, I did not cover my head with a scarf when I went for meetings and or field trips. It conflicted with my personal values. There was one time when I was on a field trip and had to meet a group of farmers in one of the remote areas that I wondered if I should. I was the only woman amidst the older grey bearded, turbaned men sitting on the ground in a circle to discuss their needs and problems. I decided against it as I felt that I would be so aware of me not being myself that I would not do justice to the meeting. I sat in my position on the floor next to the translator and after a short silence, we had a good meeting. No one left the meeting because I was a woman or did not have my head covered.

As a foreign service officer, I found that life can be lonely at times. In some places, language and cultural barriers made it difficult to make friends outside of our embassy or other donor staff. So, I learned to rely on my American colleagues for emotional and social support.

I learned being flexible is an asset. For example, in West Africa, we had to modify our programs, within our regulations, to accommodate congressionally designated special funding, for example anti-terrorism. In Armenia we figured out how best to accommodate the requests of the then all-powerful diaspora interested programs and design programs that would ultimately benefit the Armenian people. I learned that patience works, and persistence is an important skill when working in countries such as Eritrea. I learned that change takes time. But I also learned that change does happen if you work with the communities and listen to them. My work in Bangladesh in designing the family planning program was one example.

I knew that development requires a coordinated effort by many. The problems and the issues that I was working on in each country were too large to be solved by one country's assistance alone and required collaboration and coordination with many other donors and the host country. And, most of all the commitment and willingness of the host country decision makers is of utmost importance. At all my posts, I tried my best to create a donor group or some mechanism by which donors could coordinate and build on each other's resources and not duplicate efforts.

Another hard lesson for me was to discover that development is not linear. I learned to deal with disappointments and heartaches when I hear about countries that once were on the brink of economic and democratic reform, regress due to ethnic or political conflicts.

I thought I was a good manager and supervisor. I believe in teamwork, fairness and treating everyone equally. I believe in listening. I believe in mentoring. But there were other lessons. It took me some time to learn that being head of the USAID mission, people watched me for signals. Who

I would sit with at lunch, my body language to see how I reacted to something someone said or did. I learned that when I said I have an open-door policy, that I should mean it. I learned that setting examples through my actions was important to build trust and performance. I learned that apologizing and recognizing when I was wrong was helpful. I discovered that my staff liked that I would walk down the hall most mornings wishing everyone good morning – or if I could not do it in the mornings that I found time during the day. I found that as much as managing upwards was important, managing downwards was equally important for mission morale. I learned that it was in my interest never to surprise my ambassadors and learn to develop a working relationship built on professional respect with the embassy team. There were many dos and don'ts that I learned over time. Above all, I learned not to take myself too seriously and let the position get to my head. I tried to stay humble. One thing I wished I could have been better at was adding a bit of humor to my management style and learning to have more casual conversations.

As a foreign services officer, I learned how best to balance and separate my personal views from the job. I had taken an oath to do my duty as a government employee and a foreign service officer. I have worked under republican and democratic administrations. During every administration and congress, I learned to adopt and do my job, understanding that each administration brings their priorities as foreign policy goals. But I also knew that there was support for what USAID did and its role in our foreign policy interests. Thus, the decisions of the current administrations to dismantle USAID and much of U.S foreign assistance has been very hard for me to understand and come to terms with personally.

When I am asked about my work and career, I say, "I loved it." The road was not always easy, I took some detours, I made some mistakes, but in the end, I arrived where I wanted to be. And I am proud of my work and contributions. If I had to do it all over again, I would make the same choices. People say I was lucky to have had the opportunities I had, but I say to them—that the choices I made did make my luck.

PART II

EXPLORING THE WORLD

"Life is either a daring adventure or nothing at all"

Helen Keller

Summer Holidays in the Himalayas

My family took trips during summer vacations when I was a child. My father's job as the agricultural specialist in the Indian civil service required extensive travelling to monitor agriculture projects. When he was posted in Punjab, in the northern part of India, his trips often were to the mountainous regions in the Himalayas. One summer we stayed at the government guest house in Kasauli, a small city, on the way to the more popular summer resort city of Simla. I would wake up in the mornings to rooms full of mist. I walked from room to room with my arms outstretched, pretending I was flying in the clouds. On another trip, my sister and I were playing in an empty school bus parked for the night on the grounds of the guest house in Simla. My parents were still asleep. The morning sun brightened the snow peaks of the Himalayas in the background where we were playing. The fresh mountain air gave us energy to run around and chase each other until we ran into the bus and my sister shut the bus door over my hand—she said it was an accident, but I am not sure.

One summer when I was about six or seven, my mother announced that we were going for a longer trip than usual and that we would be in remote rural areas in the mountains. My father was going to Leh, the capital city of Ladakh, to inspect some agricultural projects. She said we were going toward Manali valley, which then was over twelve hours drive from Nabha, where my dad was posted. She said that there were no paved roads to Leh so we would stay for two weeks in a guest house in the Manali valley near the border of Tibet, while my dad would go on horses or donkeys to Leh for his field trip, which she said is a long trek. I had no idea where Leh was. I was excited when I looked at my atlas and saw the snowcapped mountains amidst which lay a green valley and the town of Leh. I told my mother that I wanted to go with my dad. "You are too young to take that trip," she said. I disagreed.

The packing started a week before our departure. Trunks full of clothing were packed and stacked in one of the rooms. We had to prepare for cold and warm temperatures as we were going to be in the Himalayas and temperatures can vary dramatically at high altitudes. Food rations were packed in metal boxes, lentils, spices, biscuits, tea, rice and of course flour for chapatis. Sheets, quilts and pillows were piling up next to the trunks with our belongings. I had a feeling that we were relocating. The government guest houses, located in remote areas, had sleeping cots and pots and pans in the kitchen. All other supplies the guests brought with them. There was a caretaker.

On the morning of our departure, a jeep and a military platoon truck drove up to the house in Nabha. Two drivers and two men in police uniforms were in the vehicles. In addition, we had two helpers to cook and clean who were also going with us. Our luggage was loaded in the truck. The truck had three folding cots, and I wondered if we were going to be sleeping in the truck. When I asked my mother, she said we would sleep in the guest houses where they have beds. She said that we were going to be in remote areas, and that the cots were our backup. I wanted to ask how my father, my mother, my sister and I would sleep on three small cots but was afraid to interfere with the departure preparations. Everyone was bustling about getting everything ready so we could leave as early as possible given the ten to twelve-hour drive.

Once the army truck was ready, my sister and I got in the back seat of the jeep. My mother went back and forth a few times to make sure she had not forgotten anything important. I heard her give instructions to one of the housekeepers who stayed behind to take care of the house. Once satisfied, she climbed in the jeep next to my sister and me. My father got in the passenger seat. The driver waited for a sign from the army truck driver. With a wave of the hand from the truck driver, the convoy slowly drove out of our driveway.

After we passed Manali, the road in one place was flooded, and the vehicles had to take a detour. There was a path through the pine trees that we could take and hike to our guest house, which we did. I walked most of the way but had to be carried on the shoulders of one of the staff at the end. It was cold when we got to the guest house. The caretaker built a fire to warm us while we waited for our supplies to arrive. We were still a day away from our camp site.

The next day, our jeep was driving on a winding unpaved road barely wide enough for one vehicle. At each turn, I could see the steep depth of the valley and wondered if we would survive if the jeep slipped on one of the stones on the unpaved road and rolled over into the deep ravine below. We got to our final guest house by the evening. Next morning, I watched my dad ride off in the mountains with donkeys loaded with his supplies, he and one of his staff sitting on two donkeys while the sherpas walked next to the other donkeys with the supplies. I wanted to go with him. My mother again said that I was too young. At that moment, I hated being too young.

While we waited for my dad's return, I remembered fishing in the stream nearby and falling in the water. I caught no fish. I remember playing with my sister in the green fields surrounding the guest house. I remember the fresh air. I remember flying a kite that one of the staff had brought with him. I remember looking at the horizon hoping to see the image of my dad emerge in the distance. I do not remember how long we stayed there.

A Shikara Ride at Sunset

In 1967, when I was twenty-five years old, Karen was my best friend, and I planned a vacation in Kashmir. Karen lived in New York and was taking time off to be with her boyfriend, who worked at the New Delhi Ford Foundation office. I met Karen when I was working at the Ford Foundation for a year before returning to school for my master's in social work. Neither of us had been to Kashmir but we had read about its beauty, especially the famous Dal Lake. Through a tourist agency, we rented a houseboat on the Dal Lake for a week. We could have taken a flight from Delhi to Srinagar, capital of Kashmir, but wanted adventure. We decided to go by train and road.

On an August morning, we boarded the train from the old Delhi train station to Gurdaspur. We opted to travel in the second-class women-only carriage to avoid the barrage of questions Karen, and I would face from men. We had learned from our past travels in India. Questions such as

"Are you married? Why are you travelling alone? Where are your husbands? Where are you from? How come your parents let you travel alone." On and on. The questions were so annoying. The older men would sound curious, the younger men leering.

In the women only carriage, we would most likely be left alone after two to three questions like: Are you married? Where are you from? Karen and I spoke in English and many women, especially travelling in second class, were not English speakers. Most English speakers travelled first class then, but we never travelled first class. It was the sixties, and we thought of ourselves as socialists having strong opinions about the upper class. Besides, we could not afford the price for the first-class sleeper tickets.

Dragging our duffle bags, which contained a sheet and a pillow and our clothes, we boarded the train and found our compartment. We saw two young women wrapped in colorful Punjabi dress of *salwar kameez*. They sat across from each other by the window. I could feel them watch us as we placed our duffle bags under the berths, waiting with their questions. As soon as we sat down the younger of the two, Gita introduced herself and asked for our names. Gita spoke some English and was curious as to why we were not married. Did we not want children? she inquired, as if having children was the only reason anyone would wish to marry. She was about our age and already had a two-year-old child, who was fast asleep in one corner of the cushioned seater berth. Finally, Gita turned her attention to the other lady and her baby. Karen and I had brought books and other reading material to keep ourselves busy. Besides, we always had lots to talk about amongst ourselves. Subjects such as politics, meaning of life, social conditions in the world were our favorite subjects. Sometimes we discussed books we were reading. We also talked about men.

We reached Gurdaspur at 6:00 p.m. where we transferred to the night train to Jammu. Our train was scheduled to depart at 10:00 p.m. There was a small café in one corner of the train station with a red banner showing pictures of *rotis* (chapatis), tandoori chicken, and vegetables. We realized we were hungry. We carried our duffle bags over and sat in a corner at a small plastic table with two chairs. The menu was limited to lentils, rice and rotis. There was no tandoori chicken. We had hot tea, rotis with *dal makhana*, my favorite—a popular dish in north India made up of different lentils, butter, and cream, cooked in Indian spices.

Our compartment on the train to Jammu had two berths at the bottom and two on the top.

Our reservation was for the two top berths on each side. We tucked our bags under the bottom berths and climbed up by a narrow step ladder attached to the side of the berth and waited for the other occupants, but no one else came. We were relieved to have the whole compartment to ourselves. No questions to answer. As the train left the station, we moved to the lower berths. We made our beds, a white sheet and a pillow and propped ourselves against the window to read our books. Karen spread the tourist pamphlets and guidebooks and began to plan our trip. I took out my novel *Dr. Zhivago* as I was anticipating seeing the film, which was going to be released in India sometimes later in the year. The compartment was dimly lit, with enough light to read, though not bright enough by my mother's standard for reading. The conductor, dressed in a red coat and grey pants, came shortly to check our tickets, and informed us that no one else had reserved the sleeper berths. He told us to lock the door to our compartment.

We arrived in Jammu by mid-morning. The next part of the journey was by bus. The bus stop was adjacent to the train station and our bus was leaving at 4:00 p.m. We bought our tickets. We then went to the women's bathroom to brush our teeth and wash our faces. The bus ride to Srinagar was a 24-hour trip with a night stop. We waited at the bus stop until departure time as there was no place to leave our bags. The bus station was packed with people waiting for different buses. Some waiting passengers sat on the floor as metal seats were occupied. I watched a family a few feet from us preparing for their lunch. The mother spread out a blanket on which she put her tiffin and one by one opened the boxes and laid out chapatis, a dish of vegetables, dal and rice. Her husband with the two kids sat down to have their meal just before noon. They folded their hands in a short silent prayer and then began to eat. The crowd passed around them going one way or the other. The family on their four by six blanket space focused on eating their lunch, seemingly unaware of the hustle and bustle around them.

I have no memory of the first part of the journey on the bus. I slept until the bus stopped in front of a school hall at 7:00 p.m. We were told that the rest of the road was too dangerous to drive on at night. The sleeping arrangements in the large school hall consisted of a mattress, a sheet, and a pillow. It was basic comfort, but I remember being cold. I was glad I had my own sheet and a pillow. The one on the mattress looked well used. I wish I had a blanket though. The common bathroom was down the hall. At 6:00 a.m. we were handed a steamy hot cup of tea and biscuits. It was nearly 8:00 a.m. before everyone piled onto the bus to start the remaining part of the journey.

I took a window seat and Karen sat next to me. I held my breath as soon as we started on the narrow single-lane curvy road through the ravine. I could see the river below as the bus made each turn. With every successful curve that the driver managed, we all clapped, out of relief, that we made it through another precarious turn or to congratulate the bus driver for keeping the bus on the road. We had heard stories of buses losing control and ending up in the ravine, with few survivors. The tall pine trees and rugged view of the Pir Panjal Mountain range surrounding us and the fast moving, foamy Jhelum River below was an exhilarating scene, even if scary.

We reached Srinagar at 3:00 p.m. We had been on the road for over three days since leaving Delhi. When we left the bus station, we saw the Indian Airlines office. We looked at each other and we both knew that we could not take the bus back. We walked in and bought our return tickets. We had had enough adventures. We carried our bags to a rikshaw stand to take us to our houseboat. The rickshaw puller piled our duffle bags on the seat where we would sit and asked us to climb up and sit on top of our bags. Apparently, this was the way to load luggage and passengers in a rickshaw.

At the houseboat, we were met by an elderly man who gave us the tour of the boat and some pamphlets with rules and instructions regarding the use of the place. The houseboat was furnished with red, green and yellow Kashmiri carpets, had three bedrooms and one bath plus a kitchen and a small pantry. I felt its comfort with the bright colors and rich looking carpets as soon as we entered. The houseboat keeper did not look happy at seeing us alone and asked if our husbands were going to come soon. When we said no, he made a disapproving sound and left. We never saw him again. A friendlier younger guy, dressed in the Kashmiri grey coat, pajamas, and a boat like cap, came the next day and introduced himself as the caretaker. He served us breakfast, and dinner, which was included in the rental. I do not remember the total cost per day for the houseboat.

I woke up next morning to a view of the misty blue waters with a few shikara silently moving from houseboat to houseboat. A shikara is a boat like the gondolas in Venice, except that most shikaras have an awning to provide shade from the sun. The boatman sits at the back and rows like in a canoe, rather than standing. The shikaras moved slowly, casting soft shadows in the morning sun, stopping in front of the houseboats to sell flowers, fruits, or vegetables. It was a calming sight. I learned later that families come from other parts of India and rent the houseboats for the whole summer, and others own their boats as summer homes. And many like us, rent for short time. Many of the larger houseboats had their decks decorated with beautiful arrangements of flowers.

We decided to go for a shikara ride at sunset. It is the thing to do while staying on the Dal Lake. The caretaker arranged a shikara for us. A late afternoon ride cost us 100 rupees. Our shikara was furnished with a Kashmiri carpet on the wooden floor and large cushions on the seats. I sank into the soft cushions for our trip. First, we rode by the nursery, full of popular Kashmiri flowers of hyacinths, periwinkle, marigolds, irises, roses, and jasmine. Dal Lake also had floating gardens. A piece of land floating around covered with flowers and native plants.

By the time we turned around to head back, the sun had set and lights in the houseboats were on. The shikara took us along the shoreline. Some houseboats' doors and windows were open. The decks in front were decorated with hanging lights and oil lamps, shedding long wavy reflections in the water. Some doors had woven carpets instead of curtains. In one window, I saw a woman brushing her hair. I wondered if she was getting ready to go out for dinner or settling in for the evening. Was there someone else in the room with her? Were they talking? What were they saying? I wanted to be in that room with them. The shikara moved on and I saw the profile of a man, with the light from the table lamp shining on his silver hair. Was he looking at a TV program, or reading or sitting across someone else, planning the next day? I wanted to know more. We moved on. These images reminded me of David Hopper paintings, or scenes on a stage capturing a single moment and action. The soft lights, open doors and images in the windows made the houseboats seem so warm, welcoming, and intriguing. I had a strong desire to stop the shikara and enter one of these houseboats. I wanted to be part of whatever the people were doing inside those boats and experience their lives. Our shikara moved on.

It was during this Shikara ride when for the first time I became aware of wanting to be in other places than where I was. All these years later—when I travel or I take my evening walks in Madison—I look up at houses, and the sight of an open window with lights shining on a bookshelf or a painting, makes me want to be in that room. I imagine who the people might be, what they are doing, and how it would be like to live their lives. I sometimes want to knock on their door and meet them. Once when I was driving home from our cabin in the country, I followed a car with two passengers who were talking to each other until it turned off on a narrow gravel road. I wanted to follow the car to see what kind of a house they lived in and who they were and how they lived their life in the rural landscape.

Two Evacuations

I moved to Karachi from Delhi in late 1970. My ex-husband, who worked for an international foundation, was transferred to Karachi. During the early part of 1971, he had to go to East Pakistan for business, and I decided to accompany him. There had been general elections in 1970 in which the Awami League, the main party of East Pakistan won the majority. However, the result was not accepted by the ruling party in West Pakistan. This created tension and unrest in East Pakistan, but it did not seem dangerous for us to travel as there was no official travel restrictions.

For the first week life was normal in Dhaka. I read, explored the city, and listened to music on the small radio I carried with me. At the beginning of the second week, we left for Chittagong. On our third day there, suddenly the rioting and strikes accelerated and the movement for an independent Bangladesh was in full force. We heard on BBC that Pakistan had sent an army to suppress the rioting. East Pakistan erupted in violence. We heard that there was violence against the people of West Pakistan who had settled in the East for economic reasons. We were told to stay in Chittagong until things calmed down. The hotel went into lockdown. The local families immediately left for their cities and the expats who were there on business, like us, or on a vacation, were stranded in the hotel. The hotel staff was at a minimum with most fleeing to safety.

Soon the hotel was running out of water and food. I am not sure how the manager managed to feed us. Our meals were very basic—rice and lentils. We were told to conserve water and keep our lights turned off at night. A few times, we would go to the roof for fresh air and to be outside of our rooms. On a few occasions one of the hotel staff would run to the top and tell us to get to our rooms. They said rioters were closing in on the hotel.

By then concern about my safety was a priority. Being from the Punjab part of India, I look the same as people from the Punjab part of West Pakistan. Reports of people from West Pakistan being killed in riots was in the news. The office in Dhaka was negotiating with a shipping company whose cargo ship was docked in Chittagong to take me on board to Singapore, the next stop for the ship. Unfortunately, I had left my passport back at the office in Dhaka for some administrative update regarding my entry visa. The captain did not want me on his ship without my documents.

Finally, the Prime Minister from West Pakistan decided to visit Dhaka to negotiate peace and sharing of power. The Awami Leage declared a day of calm for discussions to take place. The army was pulled back from the streets and people were asked to stay home. We took advantage of the opportunity. We made a convoy of four cars and all the expats in the hotel drove to Dhaka. Although we knew a truce was declared, we took no chances. As soon as we would see a group of young men, I would duck down to make sure they would not see my face. We were told to go straight to the airport and wait for the evacuation plane.

As we entered Dhaka, I was surprised at the damage. There were destroyed army tanks on the streets. Shops and houses had been looted and burned. The airport was packed, and people were sitting all over the floor. My passport was delivered to me at the airport. Most of the people waiting were from West Pakistan with as much of their belongings they could carry on the plane. West Pakistan was planning on sending planes to evacuate people from the west Pakistan to Karachi. Foreign embassies had negotiated with the government to allow their citizens to be evacuated to Karachi also. After two days of waiting at the airport, evacuation planes started to arrive.

I do not remember where and if we had any meals during the waiting period. I remember water passed around. I had not bathed in days, nor did I have clean clothes to change into. Once the announcement was made that our plane was ready, I was amazed at the speed with which all passengers were loaded. I felt like a piece of cargo just pushed into the plane. I took the first vacant seat I saw. I did not know when my ex-husband boarded. Once I caught my breath, I noticed that the seat next to me was occupied by a nun. Her eyes were closed, and the rosary spun with speed. Her lips moved silently with each moving rosary bead in her hand. I leaned back and closed my eyes also, but not in prayer. As soon as we were in the air at safe height, she reached into her pocket under her habit and pulled out a small flask. She took a sip and handed it to me. I assumed it was water or juice and took a big gulp. Good scotch whiskey burnt my throat, but I welcomed it.

I was happy to be back at my house in Karachi. The negotiations between the two parties failed. More troops from the west were sent to the east. India joined the war to help East Pakistan become the independent country of Bangladesh. The war extended to West Pakistan when the Indian air force began bombing Karachi port. Some bombs missed the port. One struck an oil tanker that burnt for days. We took shelter under the cement staircase when the sirens went off. We covered glass windows with blankets or painted the glass black. We lived by candlelight at night.

Finally, the American Embassy declared an evacuation for US citizens. We had twenty-four hours' notice to get ready. Everyone was allowed to bring one suitcase, and one carry on to the plane. No pets. The night before the evacuation, I packed by candlelight. I found myself sitting on the floor figuring out what I should take, knowing that there was a possibility that I would never again see the rest of my belongings. I packed the necessary legal documents, jewelry my mother had given me, and some clothes. Then, I spent the rest of the night making one album from all the pictures I had as I could not carry all of them with me. I remember being nervous, not knowing when the plane would land and when we would get the call to report to the airport. Finally, when done packing, I looked around the rooms at all the beautiful carpets we had bought and other treasures, wondering if I would see them again, but it did not matter. I do not remember being anxious or afraid. I made sure I had all that I needed in that one bag to live in Tehran, where we were being evacuated. My only worry was that my parents did not know what was happening and I could not get in touch with them. All communications between India and Pakistan were cut.

I stayed in a hotel in Tehran for several weeks. Being in Tehran was like being in some magical place. I had read about the Persian Empire and its history, about the architecture, and the Persian rugs. I went to the bazaar and enjoyed sipping tea and relishing the sight of the silky Persian rugs being unfolded and spread out one by one in front of me. Just like in a story book. Women did not cover their heads or faces. Everyone was so friendly.

Once it was determined that returning to Pakistan was not possible, the organization my ex-husband worked for negotiated a short-term contract for him to work at the International Rice Research Institute in Los Banos in the Philippines. I flew to Delhi first to see my family.

As uncertain and difficult as my time was during that period, I met two wonderful people. N and S. I met them in Los Banos. N is a pianist. I first saw them at a house party. As I walked through the door of the house, I heard wonderful music from the piano floating toward me. I could not tell if it was live or background music. Then, I saw a woman's tall upright back sitting in front of the piano. Her hair tied into a thick bun with a pin holding it together. Her hands moved smoothly back and forth on the piano keys, barely touching the keys, making music. When she finished, everyone clapped. She turned around and said something which made everyone laugh. I noticed a tall man taking pictures or a video. I learned he was her husband S. When they were introduced to me, I knew I wanted to know them more. I wanted to be their friend. Their conversation about music and the arts opened another world for me.

At first, I was intimidated by their worldly appearance and their confident demeanor. Their ability to make conversations easily, tell jokes and sound smart made me feel like a small-town girl. Luckily for me, they thought I was interesting enough to want to be my friend also. They visited me in Sri Lanka, and we saw each other frequently when I was in Ann Arbor, and when they lived in New York and later moved to Washington, DC. They were there for me when I was having a difficult time in Washington, when I was unemployed and when my dad died. When I went overseas, N and I wrote long letters to each other and later shorter emails. S helped me with financial decisions when I was later working and had saved up some money for long term investment. Their daughters are like my nieces to me. We met in 1972, and we have shared happy moments and not so happy moments in our lives; and now in our eighties we share our experiences of aging. I met them when my life was filled with uncertainty. I knew my marriage was not working, I knew that getting married was a mistake to begin with which had derailed my professional journey. I had no job prospects. I did not know where to go when I knew I would leave my ex-husband. I saw very few options at that moment. They were the good that happened to me, and I have treasured their friendship.

The Sahel

We left Ouagadougou at 7:00 a.m. on a Wednesday in 1993. I drove my two-seater four-wheel drive Mitsubishi jeep with my sister as a passenger. The others, Jeffrey and three colleagues from the American Embassy, drove a Toyota Land Cruiser. Driving through the countryside, I was struck by the women at work regardless of the time of day. I saw women cooking, cleaning their houses made from mud, feeding the animals, pounding grain with a large wood mortars and pestles or working in the fields. The men I saw, sat around the large baobab trees smoking, eating, or sleeping. There was no rest time for the women in the villages in the hot and arid climate of the Sahel.

We reached Ouahigouya by 10:00 a.m. and were ready for coffee. We stopped at a small, roadside hut with a thatched roof held together by four wood poles. The hand-painted sign that read "café" stood out in the dry sandy surroundings. A plastic table with a couple of chairs under a baobab tree looked welcoming. I saw two baguettes and some bananas on the shelf of the café. The coffee was warm water with some grains of imported instant Nescafe. We sat on the plastic chairs and remarked on how the French colonial tradition of baguettes had reached all the way into the interior of Burkina. We talked about how we could always rely on finding baguettes and bananas for lunch or breakfast when we were on field trips.

Our next stop was Koro village where we stopped at a roadside restaurant. The small shack had tables and plastic chairs laid out in two rows, and we could see the smoke and smell the aroma of the meat being grilled. Warm beer and grilled goat meat and baguettes made for a much-needed lunch. We piled back into our cars as we still had about four to five hours drive and a border checkpoint to enter Mali. As we left Koro, the road ended. Our map said there was a dirt road, about two miles long, which would connect us to the gravel road that led to the Mali border, but what we saw in front of us was a maize field. We saw a solitary man on a bike, most likely going home for his afternoon nap, and asked him about the dirt road. He shrugged and said yes it used to be here but now it is not. He volunteered to lead us to where the road used to be if we wanted to follow behind his bike.

Our two four-wheel-drive vehicles followed the old man on his rickety bike through the maize field. After crossing the field, we entered a space that looked like a picture from another planet with large black rocks shooting out of the ground. For the next couple of hours, we saw no villages or people, just flat barren land with huge rocks. My sister and I rolled down our windows, pretending we were on the moon, and sang Bollywood songs at the top of our voices. We laughed and sang louder, feeling free with all the emptiness around us.

By late afternoon we were at the Mali border. The *gendarme* (police officer) at the border crossing, which was a rope strung across two poles, waived us to the side of the road. He strolled towards us and collected our passports. Then, he disappeared into a small, dilapidated building. We waited. And waited. We could have paid a "small service fee" to speed up our paperwork, but they knew that as diplomats we were not going to pay them anything. Thus, each step of the process was further slowed.

By 5:00 p.m., we finally reached the bottom of the Bandiagara (Land of the Dogan people) cliff. The road up along the edge of the cliff was curvy and barely wide enough for a car and the gravel surface was slippery. On one turn, my back tires slipped, but I managed to control the vehicle. I was afraid to look down as to where we might have landed. Once we reached the top, the village Sangha appeared right in front of us. Suddenly from nowhere, many kids emerged and swarmed our cars, smiling with bright white teeth sparkling against their darker faces, shouting, waving, and of course wanting money. We drove slowly, with kids running alongside until we passed the gate of the only guest house in Sangha, where the kids stepped away from the cars. Our rooms were small and clean with two single beds in each room. A mosquito net made useless with too many holes framed the beds. The shower and toilets were at the end of the hallway.

We ordered steak, French fries, and beans for dinner. While the dinner was being prepared, we left for a walk through the village. The kids were a nuisance, but the hike was worth it. The wooden carved windows and doors used for granary rooms are famous in this region and I was anxious to see them. I was disappointed and a little sad to see that most of the old doors and windows had been replaced by new ones made from wood or metal. We were told that we could find the old ones in antique stores in France.

The next day, we hired a guide, Ousman, to take us for a hike to the Dogan houses built into the cliffs. He was known to be the best guide. He had a limp and used a cane. I was not sure if the cane was to help him walk or to ward off the kids and the dogs. We negotiated a price of CFA10,000. At 7:00 a.m., we left with him. For the first part of the hike we walked on top of a flat plateau made of flat black rock. No trees, no houses, just a flat black surface. The kids left us as soon as we started the hike. From the black plateau, we descended onto a narrow trail at the edge of the cliff walking in a single file. We went through two villages, Banani and Drelli, but the indigenous houses were constructed deep into the side of the plateau. We could only make out large holes and some movement inside. The guide said it would take too long to find the trails the Dogan people used to get to their homes. I was glad that no one in our group decided or wanted to get closer. I felt if tourists were welcomed, the inhabitants would not have gone to all this trouble to make trails difficult. We were on the tourist trail and by 2:00 p.m. we were back at the guest house. It was hot and the sun was harsh. I was glad that I had a big floppy hat.

We left Sangha in the late afternoon after a quick lunch of steak and French fries again and reached Mopti before sunset. We checked into a hotel, across the road from the Bani River, the principal tributary of the Niger River in Mali.

Next morning, after a leisurely breakfast consisting of cereal, croissants, and eggs, we went to the mosque and to the main market—beads, masks, handwoven bright colored blankets and material of every possible hue and shade greeted us. There were aggressive kids everywhere, all wanting to help us shop and bargain for us for a tip. We returned to the hotel, tired from the heat and the kids and the bargaining, but loaded with handwoven colorful blankets, beads and more. I was a bit overwhelmed by the market.

In the evening, we hired a pirogue (long wooden boat like a canoe, but with sails) to take us across the river to the Bozo Bar, a touristy hangout, and the best place to see the sunset, we were told. As we sipped our beers on the outdoor terrace, the sun was just setting, creating deep red shadows simmering in the water from the huge handmade sails of the passing pirogues in the harbor. The pirogues were loaded with people and goods. Below us in the harbor, people were jostling to get on and off the boats to make to their destinations. Goods, mainly vegetables, fruits, onions and fabrics were being loaded and unloaded, totally unaware of the beauty surrounding them.

After dinner, we took a taxi through the town back to the hotel. The next day, our friends returned to Burkina Faso. My sister and I and Jeff had plans to keep going for another couple of days to see Djenne. An ancient city dated back to 250 B.C., apparently one of the oldest cities in the Sahel, the North Central African semi-arid region.

Djenne is located on the Niger River Delta, known for its grand mosque. We were told that there was no way to make reservations for the night, so we should be prepared to return to Mopti, if needed. A two-hour drive each way. Our guidebook mentioned that people in Djenne rented rooms to tourists. After stopping at a few houses, we got lucky and found two rooms for the night. The house had a courtyard in the center and rooms connected around it. An older couple with their young son lived on one side of the house and rented rooms across the courtyard.

Most of the houses in Djenne were made of mud. A ladder took us to the rooftop, and I saw that rooftops of all houses on our section of the street were connected. Many rooftops were scattered with red peppers for drying, contrasting the deep red chilies against the rusty mud roofs. Sitting at the edge of the rooftop we could see the mosques in the distance. Our host negotiated a guide for us, and we took a short walk around the town and to the grand mosque. The Djenne grand mosque is an adobe mosque, the largest mud structure in the world. The original one dated back to the 13th century and was known for being the main learning center in the Sahel,

I woke up at 5:30 a.m. the next morning to take a short walk through the area where most of the smaller mosques with decorative hand paintings and carvings were located. I found these mosques far more interesting than the grand mosque. The quietness of the hour made the white painted buildings with black markings more vivid and overwhelming. I am glad I did it. I saw details on the walls that in the rush of the guided tour, the evening before, I had missed.

We left the same day and arrived back in Ouagadougou by 6:00 p.m. It was a long trip back but the extra stop in Djenne had been worth it.

Looking back, I feel fortunate to have taken this trip, and trips for example to Timbuktu and other remote places when opportunity and time allowed. I accompanied the ambassador and his wife to Timbuktu on a small four-seater Cessna plane. There was no border to cross, the pilot and owner of the plane just landed on a small earthy runway. No one checked our passports. Timbuktu once was famous as a center for trade and learning in the 15th century. Now it looked like a sleepy little village. I did find some ancient beads in a small market made up of a few stalls. Before departure, we wanted our passports stamped for memories of having been to Timbuktu. Finally, someone went looking for the customs inspector and woke him from his siesta at his house. We followed him to a small mud building. He found a stamp in a dusty drawer and stamped our passports. He said that very few tourists come to Timbuktu anymore. My trips to countries and places in West Africa, like those above and other to Tuareg markets in North Burkina, seem more memorable now because the region is not as secure as it was. I believe no tourists are allowed in many of the places that I was fortunate to have the opportunity to visit.

Almaty-Tashkent-Almaty

On the morning of February 24, 1996, I arrived at Almaty's terminal at 6:00 a.m. for my flight. I was supposed to go to Tashkent, but I could not get a seat on the direct flight to Tashkent. The alternative was to take a flight to Chimkent, located in northwestern part of Kazakhstan and from there to drive to Tashkent. The USAID office in Tashkent would send a car and a driver to pick me up.

On entering the airport, I looked at the check-in counters and did not see any signs for Chimkent. I walked toward a counter where a woman with a large *ushanka,* a women's hat common in Russia, wearing a black fur coat was sitting. A few passengers were lining up at her counter, so I joined them. When my turn came, I stepped up and saw a sheet of paper in front of her with all the passengers' names and Chimkent written on the top. I handed her my passport and ticket and without saying a word or looking up, she checked my name on the list and pointed toward a door which was closed and about 20 people waiting to enter. I asked the person in front of us if the line was for Chimkent. *"Da"* (yes). I stood in line.

An hour later—another group of people moved in front of us, the door opened, and a sign appeared on top: "Karakol" in Russian. A city in Kyrgyzstan. My line moved to another closed door, and I followed. After what seemed like a long time, the door opened though no sign appeared. We checked through the police security and moved to another waiting area. The *ushanka* wearing woman who had checked me in was standing at the door of the waiting room. Apparently, she was also our flight attendant. Finally, at noon, our flight attendant motioned the passengers toward a bus which had seats in the front and the back half of the bus was for luggage.

We were dropped off in front of a Yak, a small Russian-made plane. As I got off the bus, she motioned toward the back of the plane for me to load my bag. I had a small carry-on but was not allowed to take it on the plane. My checked bag was lined up with others besides the plane and we had to identify our bags before they were loaded onto the plane. I boarded the plane from the tail end, my first such entry to a plane. I found a window seat, sat down, leaned back and fell flat on my back. The back rest was broken. I moved to another seat and sat next to a man I thought was from Afghanistan. He turned out to be from Kyrgyzstan.

When everyone settled down, I became aware of the silence. No engines were turned on—no ground crew around the plane. But no one looked worried. I took out my Russian book. It was freezing. I looked around and everyone had their heavy coats on. My coat, which I thought was a hundred percent wool, was not warm enough. I had a woolen shawl which I wrapped tightly around me. I asked my fellow passenger, *Kagda Mbi Otxodtb?* (When will we depart?) He said, "I don't know," in English. At that point the flight attendant walked to the captain's cabin and opened the door, but no one was in there. There were some mild inquiries from the passengers as she walked down the aisle. She mumbled something in Russian which translated to "not going." My neighbor turned to face the window and went off to sleep. I looked around and many passengers were asleep. Some took out food and drinks which they had brought on board; it was lunchtime. I did not have any snacks with me, thinking I would get something on the plane.

Time passed. One passenger got off the plane to smoke and came back with the information that Chimkent was amidst a snowstorm, and nobody knew when we could leave. There were no grunts of disappointment or complaints. People just turned over in their small seats and continued sleeping, eating, and drinking. Finally, at 2:30 p.m., I heard a commotion at the rear of the plane and saw three crew members boarding and marching right through the plane to the front. No words of explanation. It was our pilot, co-pilot, and the engineer.

The takeoff was smooth as Almaty had clear skies. However, within fifteen minutes into the flight, we entered the bumpy snow skies. It was a rough ride. All I could see out of the window was one big thick wall of whiteness. There were no announcements and once we started the descent and the landing gear came down with a thud, I was nervous about landing as I could not see the ground. The wheels hit the runway at what seemed like a faster speed than normal. Finally, when we came to the parking place, the engines were turned off and I thankfully got ready to get up to leave. My neighbor said, "we have to wait". Wait for what? I thought. We had been waiting all day. I sat down. After 20 minutes, the pilot, the co-pilot and the engineer came out of the cabin, marched down the aisle, without a look or a word and got off the plane. Then all passengers got up to disembark. We stumbled out of the small plane, and I collected my carry on which was deposited at the bottom of one of the wings. It was still snowing.

On walking out of the terminal, I saw a big heavy-set man wearing a *kufi* (Uzbek hat) holding a USAID sign. I was so relieved that I nearly hugged him. We got into a *Lada*, the popular Russian made car and left the airport in blizzard conditions. Fifteen minutes outside of Chimkent, he stopped on the side of the road. I thought he needed to wait as we could not see the road from the land around. It was all covered in snow. He said he needed gas, but I saw no gas station. He took two jerry cans and walked to a gas truck parked down the road and started filling his can. He told me that gas is cheaper in Kazakhstan. I saw a few other trucks parked beside the road and cars stopping to fill their jerry cans with gas. We moved on slipping and sliding. Driving through the flat white land, I saw hazy outlines of farmhouses and sheep and horses. We could barely make out the road. Finally, at 5:30 p.m., we rolled into Tashkent. On the way, the driver had pointed out a large arch gateway which marked our entry to Uzbekistan. There was no border crossing to stamp my passport.

The office staff was waiting for me and informed me that I had to go to the airport to get my visa before I could check into the hotel. So off I went to the airport. I was told that the immigration staff at the airport had all the papers, and they were waiting for me. I got to the airport and the door to the immigration office was closed and no one was in sight. Finally, after an hour a uniformed man showed up in the hallway and my wonderful driver asked if he was the visa officer. In ten minutes, he gave me a multiple entry visa. At 8:00 p.m. I checked in at the TATA hotel. I was starving—all I had eaten was a banana and a cup of tea before leaving my apartment in Almaty at 5:30 a.m. I knew then that I had a lot to learn and prepare for my travels in Central Asia.

TATA hotel was one of the few hotels approved by the US Embassy. I checked in and was told to go to the third floor where I would get my key. On exiting the elevator, I saw a woman bundled up in a long coat sitting behind a desk which resembled a tiny kiosk. It had, beside the row of room keys, biscuits, cigarettes, packets of chips, small bottles of soft drinks, and vodka. She handed me my room key. My room was bare of any decoration and had two narrow beds, a small TV, and a bathroom equipped with toilet paper, a small towel, and a piece of soap. I thought there had been a mistake. I went down and asked to change rooms. My request was met with a strange look from the receptionist. I was told that all the rooms are the same. One of the staff behind the reception desk said quite seriously, "This hotel was built by an Indian businessman, and in India they are small people." I was too tired to respond. I returned to my room.

It was still snowing when the office car picked me up the next morning to go to work. I saw women in oversized coats with long brooms clearing the snow from the streets. It Reminded me of the play "Slavs". The apartment buildings had colorful patterns in traditional Uzbek designs either painted or fitted with colorful tiles. I was in Tashkent for a week to cover for our USAID coordinator, who was on leave.

During the weekend, I visited the museum. I bought a rug, and the office arranged for me to visit the house of a master ceramist, Akbar, who lived in one of the mahallas, an area of houses traditionally built around familial ties. Most of the mahallas were in the older part of the city. The car stopped in front of a huge wooden gate with mosaic designs. I walked in through a small door which was cut into the larger gate, like a window. The main gate, I was told, was for cars but was seldom used. Akbar's assistant met me and we, along with my interpreter, walked down a driveway covered by a carved wooden canopy on both sides and above. The driveway led to the courtyard which was surrounded by rooms on all four sides.

I met Akbar in the courtyard. He came towards me with folded hands and said "*Assalomu alaykum*." Uzbek greeting. He gave me and my interpreter the tour of the house. We first saw the room with the original kilims and equipment that his father used. He then showed us the museum room on the second floor with the family's pottery collections. Most of these pieces were not for sale. Finally, he took us to the show room where I bought two plates, and a fruit bowl made by Akbar.

He invited us to have chai (tea). The chai turned out be a spread of Uzbek nuts and traditional sweets and dates with *Obi Non* and *lepeshka* (Uzbek breads). I felt like I was in a national Geographic documentary! The room was full of carpets and family collections including Russian chandeliers. His wife and daughter joined us. We chatted a bit about the changes since independence. One big change he said was that more and more men and women have started to follow the Muslim traditions that were not allowed before. I asked him what he thought about his sons, daughters, and wife fasting during Ramdan, something not allowed under the Soviet system. He said that himself he did not fast, and he did not give an opinion, but did say that more of the young, especially men, are turning to religion. I noticed that his wife and his daughter had their heads covered with a bright printed scarf.

The weather was sunny during my trip to Tashkent, until the day of my departure. I woke up to another snowstorm. We called the airport and were told that the airplane had left Almaty and that I should come to the airport. I arrived at the airport at 11:00 a.m. for my 1:00 p.m. flight. My check-in was uneventful, and after passing through security, I settled into the waiting room, which consisted of a wide corridor with mostly broken benches lined up along the wall. Some white plastic chairs were scattered around. A kiosk which read "Café" was closed, but a plastic table with chairs was set up in front of it and few people sitting and waiting, I assumed, for the café to open. There were six passengers already waiting for the Almaty flight. I pulled out one of the chairs, propped my feet on one of the broken benches, got comfortable and took out my Russian book. It was freezing cold. There was no heat. But I was better prepared for the wait this time. I had all my woolen gear with me.

It was past 1:00 p.m. and there was no action. No one knew where our plane was. There were four airport security staff, who did not look concerned. They sat around a plastic table and started to play cards. At about 2:00 p.m. the snow stopped, and the café was opened by a young woman in a red skirt and sweater. The passengers cheered. More and more passengers piled into the hallway. Over the next four hours, some flights arrived and took off. At boarding time, one of the security staff would stop playing his card game, mumble something, walk up to the end of the room, and open the half side of the steel door which was locked with a padlock. Passengers would rush up to the door, afraid that it would be locked again, and pass through to the waiting bus. As soon as the last person passed through, he would shut and lock the door, put the key in his pocket and return to his card game. The hall would empty for a while, except for us six waiting for the Almaty flight. Then people would stream in again. I noticed that a small group of passengers arrived between flights and sat down. After some time, someone said something about the flight number and there was commotion and panic. Apparently, they had been a little late and not realized that the passengers had already boarded. These few passengers started banging on the steel door and running around trying to find the person with the key. The card players shrugged and said they did not know where he was. Finally, with some running around and yelling, the person with the key strolled back and let the passengers out. I could see them running on the tarmac toward the plane. Back in the hallway, everyone turned back to whatever they were doing.

By 7:00 p.m. everything had become quiet and six of us, the Almaty passengers, were still waiting. I thought that I would warm myself with a little vodka. I had seen other passengers buy some from the café. I walked up and asked for a shot of vodka and was told with a look of disbelief that I had to buy a bottle. I returned to my seat without the vodka.

One of the Almaty passengers asked whether they knew what the problem was. The response was "we know nothing." I was afraid that we might have to spend the night there. I tried to call the duty officer at the Embassy but had no connections. Finally, at 10:30 p.m., I heard a voice calling "Almaty". The three of us foreigners were asked to follow and were driven to board the twenty—seater prop plane. We took our seats and waited. It was so cold. The flight attendant and the crew who were sitting at the back of the plane pulled up the steps and closed the door. There we were in this dimly lit plane, below freezing temperatures, waiting for the other three passengers. I had put on all my layers of clothes—silk undershirt, turtleneck, sweater, and a coat. I put on another pair of socks. I took out my woolen shawl and wrapped it around myself. I put on my gloves and a hat and sat on the plane and waited.

There were no ground staff around the plane. I saw the bus drive up, but not seeing the steps down, it left again—maybe thinking it was not the right plane. It was still snowing. After fifteen minutes the bus returned, circled the plane, and stopped. I saw the passengers get off and walk around the plane looking for the steps. I looked back and saw that the flight attendant was not even looking out. I pointed and said *"passanzhir"* (passengers). Finally, around 11:00 p.m., we took off. Of course, when we landed at Almaty twelve hours later, we had to wait until the crew had disembarked, before we could leave the plane. I was getting a little taste of what life had been like under the Soviet system.

Field Trips in Afghanistan

Field trips in Afghanistan were logistically complicated. I had to get security clearance for each work trip outside the compound and the site had to be cleared to ensure safety. Once I had clearance from our security office, I had to wear a bullet-proof vest and a helmet. I hated that part, as none of it fit my small stature. I was uncomfortable all the time, adjusting and readjusting, during the drive and until I reached my meeting place and was inside the doors. Field trips outside of Kabul had the same routine, but I had to give longer notice to our security office. All out of Kabul trips were by helicopter.

I remember my first trip outside of Kabul. I was invited by our USAID staff posted at the Nuristan Provincial Reconstruction Team (PRT), a team made up of military and civilian staff to help improve stability in a particular region where the PRT was. I was told that the helicopter would not touch the ground and would hover a few feet above and we had to jump out. In my ill-fitted military gear, I was nervous, but it turned out to be easier than I had feared. I stood at the edge of the door and as the helicopter got close to the ground, I jumped onto a platform. This was my first visit to a PRT. It was a military camp much like I had seen in the movies. I met with the senior army official in charge of the base, for security briefing and planning the field trip. Our USAID representative at the PRT made all the logistical arrangements.

On the first day, I was going to visit a road construction project and meet with the farmers who would benefit from having a road to their villages and fields. After breakfast in the canteen, we gathered near the Humvees ready for the trip. The military men and women gathered in a circle holding arms much like a soccer team. The priest said a short prayer for everyone's safety. It was part of the routine before every trip in the field. Our convoy consisted of six Humvees. I had never been in an armored Humvee before. They look so big from the outside, but inside with all the protective gear and guns on top, it's a tight space. We drove for about two hours to get to the place where construction was in progress. There was not a moment during that trip when my body was relaxed. I expected a mine or two to go off any moment. I saw men standing around or sitting in front of their houses in the villages we passed, they stared at us, but no one waved, as they would in other countries when I visited our project sites. I wondered if they were with us or with the Taliban.

On the second day, we were going to a village which I was told was not a conflict area and we went in a regular military vehicle, with one security vehicle in advance to screen the area. I entered a house where the advance team had gathered the women for our conversation. It took a little while for women to warm up. They had designated an older man, out of cultural respect and practice, to speak for them. The women would talk to him first in the local language and he would relay their message to us and the interpreter would translate to me in English. Soon, the women realized that he was not really relaying what they were saying, and they asked him to leave. After the elderly gentlemen left, we had more of an open discussion about their needs. Child welfare was top on the list. Most of the women wanted some economic opportunity. They wanted literacy programs for them and their children, many who could not go to school during the conflict. We were all sitting on the floor, which is common in rural Afghanistan houses. US protective female military personnel stood at the door with a rifle. It was hard for me to relax and have a conversation. I finally asked if she could join us, she refused, but did sit down which made it less distracting for me. Over time I got used to having security staff around me when I was out of the compound.

On the way back from that trip, I was sitting in the helicopter across from a fully armed security person. We were flying low, for reasons that were not explained to me. I could look out and see the rugged mountains and I kept thinking about what the security guard would do if we were shot at. I was afraid and was making promises to my mother in my head that I would never do something like this if I came out alive from Afghanistan. I remember being so happy at seeing the helicopter landing site at our compound.

Another of my trips to Bamiyan was somewhat different. The Bamiyan province was relatively secure at that time, and we did not have to travel in armored vehicles. I had wanted to go to Bamiyan. I wanted to see the cliffs where the ancient carved Buddha statues were destroyed by the Taliban in 2001. USAID supported an agriculture project, and I was scheduled to meet with the recipients, all men to assess how the project was benefiting them. On arriving at the site, I saw a large tent with about twenty to thirty Afghan men sitting around. I walked under the tent and sat down next to the moderator of the meeting who also translated for me. I was the only women amongst twenty or thirty older men with loosely tied turbans and long beards sitting in the circle on the floor which was covered with beautiful rugs. It was a bit intimidating. The meeting was slow to start. No one spoke. I waited. A two-year-old toddler crawled over to me. I am not sure where he came from. I looked around and saw no Afghan women. That child gave me an opening, and I started asking the men about their families, children, and their health status. Soon, the men were talking about shortages of seed, fertilizer and how difficult it was to work and live in the conflict environment. All during the meeting, the thought that any one of them could be a Taliban supporter never left me. At the end I looked up and saw our security staff at some distance but maintaining their vigilance. I had forgotten that they were there during the meeting.

I had requested to visit the cliffs where the Buddha statues once existed. The place of our meeting with the farmers was on one of the surrounding hills and at the end of the meeting, I walked to the edge and in the distance could see the large holes where once the statues had been. On our way to the Buddha site, we drove through green valleys, and I could understand why in literature the area is called the "Valley of Gods." Walking through the site and standing in one of the large holes from which a Buddha statue once looked out at the valleys, I could understand why the site was selected for the statues and wondered why the Taliban had to destroy them. We climbed the hill and walked around the caves with the vast openings where the statues had been. It was so peaceful.

Tennis in Playa del Carmen

In March, Gud and her husband Jeffrey arrived in Playa Del Carmen from Madison. It was their second trip to Playa. She woke up, had coffee, and headed to reserve a court in a large public sports complex for tennis on Tenth Avenue, a few blocks from her hotel. The tennis courts are available to the public from 8:00 a.m. to 4:00 p.m. It gets extremely hot after noontime. Thus, most players prefer the morning hours.

For Gud, reserving the tennis court was the most important activity of the mornings in Playa. She woke before Jeffrey and walks over when the office at the stadium opens. The court can be reserved only one day in advance and for only one hour at a time by any one person for singles or doubles. As she approached the tennis courts, she recognized Bill and his wife Sue, who were already on the court, playing with a group.

Gud had met Bill and Sue. They were from Canada and visit Playa for three months every winter. They were friendly and loved tennis. Playa was the best place they discovered to have access to public tennis courts; they told Gud. At six feet tall, Bill could be intimidating when playing tennis and he was extremely competitive. His wife Sue was on the quiet side and much shorter. She was a more consistent player and more fun to play with. Gud and Jeffrey enjoyed playing with them, often joining them for a beer afterwards at one of the restaurants on Fifth Avenue. She was glad to see them on the court and was hoping for some fun doubles matches with them.

In choosing a winter vacation destination, Gud and Jeffrey had researched places like Costa Rica, Puerto Rica, St. Johns and both coasts of Mexico. They wanted a place that met their winter vacation needs. She wanted the sun and the beach; Jeffrey could only be in the sun for ten minutes a day. His pale Norwegian skin burned quickly. She loved the sea; he did not. He loved to bike; she did not. But they both liked history and archelogy, and hiking and walking. They both loved playing tennis. They both liked people-watching and international cuisine. They both also wanted local character when they go to a place for a vacation. When they were younger, they used to go to exotic places, like India, Sri Lanka, or Thailand because such places offered a bit of everything that they both like to do together. As they got older and the long flights and jet lag got to be too much to handle, they looked for places in the same time zone as Wisconsin. Thus, they settled on Playa Del Carmen. They felt they had found a perfect getaway from the harsh Wisconsin winters, and found a city that met their vacation needs, especially tennis.

Gud walked in the office and looked at the reservation book. The courts were reserved for the whole week from 8:00 a.m. until midday. She recognized Bill and Sue's names and names of the Canadian friends on the register. The women behind the desk, who spoke some English, said that the policy had changed, and players could reserve a week in advance. "Come early next Monday to sign up," she said.

Gud complained that reservations should not be allowed that far in advance because it is not fair to other players who do not have a large group or might have shorter visits.

"I understand, but I do not make the rules," the woman said.

The following Sunday, Gud lay awake at night waiting for the alarm to go off so that she could, walk over and be the first in line. She was a few minutes late again and saw that the Canadians had already reserved all the courts and were playing on both courts. She was disappointed but thought maybe they could play with Bill and Sue, like before.

She walked to the courts. "Hello, good to see you," Bill called to her between his serves.

Gud waited until the tennis game was over and Bill and Sue and their two friends walked up to the side to get some water.

"I see you have both courts reserved for the week," Gud said. "Maybe we can play with you all."

"Not today, we have enough players for two courts," Bill responded quickly. Gud noticed that Sue was about to say something but stopped.

"It doesn't have to be today; we can join you tomorrow or the day after. We are here just for two weeks and would really like to get some tennis in," Gud said.

"Maybe next year. We have enough people." Bill responded offhandedly.

Gud turned around and left the court without another word, fuming. What had happened to the friendly Bill and Sue, who'd said how much they enjoyed playing with us last year? Gud returned to the hotel and vented to Jeff about how unfriendly Bill had been.

Jeff told Gud to relax and reminded her that she came for a vacation and that they could play later. That was not the issue with her anymore. Tennis was one of the main reasons they came to Playa. Plus, it seemed unfair. She was determined to take the courts back from the Canadian tennis mafia.

Next morning, Gud went to the tourist head office and complained about the Canadian group taking over the courts. She mentioned that some other players who were waiting for the courts were also complaining. She was told that they would monitor the signup sheet more closely. Gud and Jeffrey tried to play tennis in the afternoon, but the heat was unbearable, especially for Jeffy who was recovering from his heart attack earlier in the year. After two weeks, with little tennis, Gud and Jeff returned home disappointed. They made plans for next year hoping that the rules and policy would be changed.

The next year when Gud and Jeff visited Playa, she went to the sports complex to sign up for tennis. There was no change, and the courts were all reserved for the week by the Canadians. Frustrated, she decided not to let tennis spoil her trip, but she did put in a written complaint this time to the tourist office. She felt she had to do something.

Gud decided to explore Playa with Jeff. They walked up and down the high-end touristy street. Fifth Avenue was lined with boutiques, souvenir shops and restaurants offering Italian, Greek, and Mexican food. There was no shortage of bars to sit in and enjoy a drink with salsa and chips and people watch. When overwhelmed by watching fashion and beautifully suntanned bodies, and indulging in mojitos and margaritas, they went to 30th Street and beyond where they found a whole different world made up of budget travelers and Mexican restaurants filled with Mexicans.

Gud bonded with Jeff over walking instead of tennis. In the mornings, they discovered a route on Fifth Avenue away from downtown all the way to the outskirts of the town. That part of Fifth Avenue was quiet and not developed with touristy apartments and condos, shops and cafés. She and Jeff chit chatted about nothing as they walked. Not something they did often.

The beach was two blocks from the hotel, and they spent days on the beach, often taking long walks as far as Esmeralda beach—a four-mile walk, difficult but good for the feet on the warm sand. Jeff made sure that he put on enough sunscreen and a T-shirt and a hat to avoid sunburn. Some days, they rented some chairs and lay in the sun watching the beach scene, with kids playing in the sea and others tossing volleyballs to one another. On the weekend, they planned a trip to Coba and Telum to see the ruins. They went to Cozumel twice for snorkeling and on one trip rented a Jeep to go around the island to see the Mayan Ruins of San Gervasio. Gud and Jeff saw a lot of the city and surroundings when not thinking about tennis.

The following year Gud talked to her tennis friends in Madison about Playa. For some time, they had discussed taking a tennis holiday together. Her talk about tennis, good beaches and Fifth Avenue food was an enticing sales pitch. When she told them about her efforts to take back the tennis courts from the Canadians, their enthusiasm doubled. So, six tennis players from Madison boarded the plane in February. She thought to herself, "Canadians, be warned, the Americans are coming."

Gud woke up the first morning after arrival and excitedly walked to the sports complex. The office opened at eight thirty in the morning, and she was there at 8:00 a.m. She was surprised to see that both courts were free. She reserved one court leaving the other open for other players. She returned to the hotel and over breakfast announced that the Canadians were missing, much to everyone's disappointment. They had entertained themselves with various scenarios of outdoing the Canadians and taking the courts back from them. Gud and her friends played tennis every morning for a week. She wondered if Bill and his group might be out touring.

Next Monday when Gud went to the office to sign up, she expected to see the courts reserved by the Canadians. To her surprise, that was not the case. Although, she loved having the court to themselves, the mystery of what happened to the Canadians gnawed at her. They had been such regulars for so many years. She hoped that all was okay with them.

Then, one evening Gud and Jeff walked to the beach bar where she knew the Canadians would often gather after playing tennis. She and Jeff got a table and ordered a beer, wondering if the Canadians would show up. After about half an hour, she saw two people walking up to the bar. She recognized Bill and Sue, and she waved to them. She noticed that Bill was using a cane. Gud invited them to sit with her and Jeff.

"Are you okay, what happened?" Gud asked after they had ordered their drinks. Bill said that he had fallen playing tennis and broken his ankle. Jill added, "he was going for a ball he should have let go—after all we're not young anymore. He's too competitive."

Gud tried to sound sympathetic and asked about the others. Bill said they had not come as he had not been able to organize the trip due to his surgery.

Sue was going to say more, but Bill spoke first and asked if Sue could join Gud and Jeff as Sue would love to play.

Gud looked at Bill and nearly said, "We have

enough people as our friends from Madison came with us this year, maybe next year."

But instead, she said, "Sure, we can take turns. How about tomorrow."

Sue smiled and thanked Gud. Bill said nothing.

After finishing their drinks, Gud and Jeff paid and with a "see you tomorrow" to Sue, stood up to leave.

Jeff turned to Gud and said, "We should walk back on the beach, or do you want to walk on Fifth Avenue?"

Gud decided to take the shorter route via Fifth Avenue to get to the hotel sooner to share the news with her Madison friends.

PART III

BEING A WOMAN

"There are two powers in the world; one is the sword, and the other is the pen. There is a third stronger than both, that of women"

Malala Yousafzai

At the Mela in Old Delhi

I met Karen in July 1966, when I was working as a receptionist in the Ford Foundation in Delhi. I was taking a break from studies after my undergraduate. I had given myself time to make a little money, see India, and figure out what career path to take.

One day, Karen walked into the office and introduced herself with no hesitation, as if I should have been expecting her. She had a head of straight dark brown hair that fell to her shoulders and friendly light brown eyes looking directly at me. She was wearing a summer flowery dress and carrying a backpack. I immediately liked her.

"I just arrived from Berkeley," she said. "Can I see Gene?"

Gene worked at the Ford Foundation as a research assistant and had mentioned that a friend might visit for the summer. That summer visit lasted for two years, and Karen and I became good friends and traveling companions. Karen, a social worker, in addition to wanting to see India, also did volunteer work for a center for the homeless children.

Karen and I liked to spend our free time together. One weekend, we decided to visit a fair, *Mela* in Hindi, that was held annually in an open field near the Red Fort in Old Delhi. We had met two Peace Corps volunteers who had just arrived in Delhi and decided to show them around town. Karen and I met at the office and took a bus to the *mela* grounds where we were meeting our new friends. As we entered, I saw that the Ferris wheel was packed. Kids were screaming as the upper passenger carriage swung downwards. Bright red and yellow colors from the saris women wore splashed against the sky as the Ferris wheel rotated.

We had agreed to meet our friends near the food stalls. Every *mela* has an area where food, such as chat, chicken tikka, and of course ice cream, is located. To find it, all you need to do is to follow the aroma of the chicken, covered with spices, floating from the charcoal grill. Walking toward the food area, we passed rows of stalls selling the latest fashion clothes, soaps, Indian oils, and household decorative items. We wanted to stop to look, especially at the boutique stores, but decided to wait until after we had met our friends.

As we approached the food mart, we saw our friends at the chicken tikka stand. It was hard to miss them, two blonde, six feet tall and white men among the darker and shorter crowd around them. Blond hair is uncommon in India and everyone around was staring at our friends. We ordered two plates of chicken tikka and four nans. There was no place to sit, so we ate standing up, like everyone one else. Once we were done eating, we each got a bottle of Coca Cola, our favorite drink in those days, and moved a little distance to find some open space to discuss what we wanted to do next.

As we were talking, a group of men began to circle around us. I did not pay much attention, thinking they were just curious about my white, blond Peace Corps friends. The circle got larger as more men joined in and slowly, they started to close in on us. Some of the men started saying in English, "Leave your friends, come hang out with us! What do they have that we don't? We can give you a good time."

Two policemen arrived and tried to break up the crowd with their batons, but they were pushed aside as the circle of men surrounding us kept moving us in one direction and another, now shouting obscenities in Hindi and English. I realized that we had become separated from our Peace Corps friends and the policemen were nowhere to be seen. It was only Karen and me inside the circle of men. Suddenly, one of the men boldly reached out and touched Karen's back and then her breast. Then it was free for all.

The circle of men, in a wave like movement, moved Karen and me toward a covered area against a wall near the entrance, touching and grabbing our bodies as we stumbled backwards against a wall, their hands grasping at whatever part of our clothing and our body they could reach. We had nowhere to run. I remembered reading somewhere that looking into the eyes of the attacker helps and not showing fear can be a deterrent. I started shouting the worst curse words I knew in Hindi at them. I kept telling Karen in English, to keep looking at them and do not look down or cry. We tried to hit back, but there were too many. It did not seem to work, but I knew that we had to fight back.

Then, from nowhere we saw four arms reaching above the circle of men. We heard a male voice call out, "Grab our hands."

I was not sure if the arms were there to help or if they would bring more danger. But we had no choice. I shouted to Karen at the top of my voice to do what they were asking. I felt two strong hands grab my arms and drag me through the mass of bodies. I saw Karen being helped by another man. After we had cleared the circle of men, we ran to a parked car not far away at the side of the road. The car door opened, and I saw the man ahead of us who had Karen in his hold push her in the car and went around to the passenger seat. The man with me was close behind and similarly pushed me in and got in the driver seat, and the car moved away. I was sitting on a lap of an older women. Karen was sitting in the middle, crying in shock and fear. A woman sitting on the other side of the back seat was calming her while reprimanding us for being by ourselves and without our husbands. I remember the words "without your husbands" clearly while they were trying to comfort us. And then uncontrollable tears started streaming down my face.

I met Karen the next day and we talked about our experience and what nearly happened. The shock and fear stayed with us for some time, and we avoided crowds. For some months the memory of that day would make us go quiet amidst a conversation and sometimes we would get teary eyed and hold hands for comfort. I did not tell my family. I did not want to be reprimanded. Our Peace Corps friends apologized for leaving us in the crowd, but they said they had no control of the situation and tried to get to the police officer but got lost in the crowds of the mela. They tried to find us but eventually went home, a bit shaken, they said. Karen and I never saw them again.

All these years later, I am still afraid to think of what would have happened if those men had not come to help us. For a long time after, I avoided crowded areas. In theaters, I would wait until the last person left the hall before exiting. That incident made me aware of my vulnerabilities as a woman. I understood for the first time, how some men saw me. I was horrified that we came so close to being gang raped, possibly killed, in broad daylight, at a fair with thousands of people around us. The clawing hands remain fixed in my memory.

After that day, something changed in me. I started to pay more attention to how men behaved. I notice how they talk like they were entitled to everything. The way they walk in the street like it belongs to them, the way they walk practically through women in a store or the street without an "excuse me". I notice the long tiring monologues that men are not aware of but continue like it is their given right to speak. I notice how men feel they must sum up a point a woman has made just to make sure it is understood, giving it affirmation. I notice how unaware men are of their conversational dominance in a group. I notice how men initiate conversations in social settings that best meet their interests and how they control the conversation. I notice how often men sit or stand with their legs spread, taking up space. I notice in many cultures boys are encouraged to be lawyers, engineers and more, but often not the same for girls. I notice how boys' bad behavior is explained by "boys will be boys." To this day, I am sensitive to the looks that women and girls get on the street from passing men. They might be innocent looks, but my body tells me otherwise.

Karen and I took many other trips in India during her two-year stay. We learned from that one experience and were always on guard in crowded areas. But it did not deter us from going to other melas and fairs which are a part of Indian holidays and celebrations. When Karen returned to the US, I would visit her wherever she lived. Karen visited me in all the countries I was posted to. I met Karen when she was 25, and we remained close friends until she died at the age of 65. I lost my soulmate. The incident at the mela created a shared bond between us, which we did not speak about often in later years. We both knew what could have happened.

A Night on the Train

When I was writing the Mela piece, a memory surfaced that I had suppressed or pretended had not happened.

I was twelve years old, and my breasts had started to show. I was on the night train returning to Delhi after the summer holidays with my parents. A close friend of the family we knew as "uncle" was entrusted to chaperon us. A two-berth compartment was reserved for us. I was sleeping on the lower birth. My younger sister took the berth across from me. The uncle spread his bedding on the floor of the compartment between us. He locked the door from inside as the train started to move. He asked us if we were comfortable and kindly wished us good night. I went to sleep as did my sister.

I felt a hand on my breast. As soon as I moved, it disappeared. I looked around; I looked down. The uncle lay on his side on his bedding on the floor, I could not tell if he was asleep. I thought perhaps I had a bad dream and went back to sleep. Sometime later, I woke up again shaking as a hand cupped my breasts. I jerked and sat up. It was dark in the compartment, and I do not remember seeing anything. But I knew it was him. I was shivering. I looked at my sister on the berth across. I crept out of my bed and went and sat on her berth.

I sat up all night until the train reached Delhi at 6:00 a.m. and my grandfather was there to pick us up. I felt cold. He was concerned that I had a fever. I went home and got into bed and did not get up for three days.

I did not know what had really happened or what to say or to whom. I knew that I would not be believed. The uncle was such a trusted person in the house. A few days later he visited, as he often did. While sitting around the dining table, he joked about how I was afraid of the night in the train and stayed awake all night sitting up. I wanted to scream—instead I went quietly to my room.

Looking back, I realize that worse could have happened. But something changed in me at the age of twelve. I realized that as a girl I was not safe in the world. But at that time, I did not know who to trust and whom to tell and if I would be believed.

Over the years, the more I talked to friends, I learned that there are many homes where uncles, good friends of family and even fathers, take advantage of young girls knowing that they would never tell. Women friends have shared stories of workplaces where they did not feel safe, were not prepared for sexual attacks for which they had not given consent and did not believe that they will be taken seriously if they complained or told their supervisors. Much has changed since I was young, but there is much more to be done.

My purpose for sharing my experience is to show that what happened to me can happen in any family. I am hoping that mothers and fathers reading this can build trust with their daughters so that the daughters feel safe talking to them and not be afraid that they will not be believed. I am hoping that parents will believe in their daughters, support them, and get the help that they might need. I want young women in my family to never have to feel that it was their fault.

I am also hoping that parents reading this will talk to their sons early and teach them to listen to girls and women. I would like to eliminate the "boys will be boys" attitude so prevalent in so many societies.

Being a Woman in the Workplace

When I attended my first mission directors meeting in 2001, an annual event, I noticed that out of some eighty-five directors, only eighteen were women, and of those eighteen, only three were women of color. When talking to this small group of senior women managers, I heard some common themes. That, the white male network dominated the agency's systems and practices which made it easier for white men to rise in the ranks. Women had to work twice as hard to prove themselves as professionals. That USAID was less forgiving of women managers. Women heard things like, she is too aggressive, she is a screamer, she does not treat subordinates well. Such impressions right or wrong made it to the hallway gossip, affecting their reputation and in some cases careers. Similar talk about men managers was often overlooked, especially by male white managers. The women directors shared examples of their own experiences.

Listening to my colleagues, I knew that I

could not change the whole system myself, but I made a commitment to encourage and mentor women who had leadership qualities to take on senior level positions. I have continued to pursue this commitment after retirement by participating in the mentoring program that is managed by the USAID Alumni Association. Listening to the women mentees, I am discouraged that senior women managers often still struggle with their male supervisors.

During and after my career, I discovered that women often are hard on themselves in viewing their own performance. As a supervisor working with men and women to plan and guide them through their career moves, I would often hear from women that they were not sure if they were ready for a senior management position or doubted if they had the right skills. Men seldom expressed such doubts even when they were not the best performers.

I am often asked, mostly by women colleagues, about how it was working as a woman in male dominated countries. My personal experience was that my position and the fact that I was representing the US government when negotiating or being in meetings was key. Thus, during my interactions with the counterparts, I would never let myself think about how I should behave as a woman, or at five feet feel tall feel handicapped in any way. When, I would walk in the room, I would put my hand out to shake, with some authority, without hesitation or giving any vibes that I am short, a woman of color and would get down to business. I always had my position and my role at meetings in mind. I made it a habit to stick to the agenda and keep the meetings short and to the point. I am not good at small talk. That worked for me. Dealing with men in male patriarchal countries overseas was easier being in an official capacity, representing the US government as our resources were needed, I discovered. I never felt compromised or patronized by my male counterparts overseas. On the contrary I got some feedback that my business-like, no-nonsense approach was respected. What they thought privately, I did not worry about. Socially, however, it was a different story. At receptions and other social events, I had a harder time as a woman to join male groups that would naturally form around common interests and familiarity. But there were enough women managers in the embassy and the donor community for me to socialize with.

However, navigating the male dominated environment at home in the US was complicated and a learning experience. I noticed men spoke more in meetings. Some had the need to say something every time to the point that at one meeting, I got so tired of listening to this one person who raised his hand at every question to share his opinion that without being conscious, I just said, "J. always has something to say."

People around were surprised, but then there was laughter. I was embarrassed, but not sorry I said it. I did notice a change after that when the moderator would make sure that he noticed the hands of women that were raised, which he had overlooked before.

I also noticed men spoke over women. Men in meetings would support other men's position and viewpoint. For example, when one of them was making a point, another would often start his point by saying, "as J was saying" or "I agree with J and want to add..." I noticed men did not do the same when a woman made a point and worse still, I noticed that women did not do the same for women.

In Ann Arbor, a friend of mine and I were the only women in a class of all white men taking a course in the school of management. In small group discussions, whenever notes needed to be taken, men would look at us to take the notes. The first time my friend picked up her pen and started to take notes. I kept quiet.

The next time, when my friend picked up her pen, I said, "No, we will take turns."

The men did not like it, but I was not there to make friends. I was afraid that at the next meeting they would be asking us to get their coffee.

At the beginning of my career, during senior level meetings, I would not speak up. I would have questions or viewpoints, but I would not be sure if they were important enough to raise. Then, someone else, often a male, would speak up with the same questions and I would be sitting at the table thinking, why did I not raise my hand? I noticed that I became invisible to others. I had a good reputation as a solid professional, hardworking, straightforward, fair and smart so why was I hesitant to speak up. I had to change that. I realized that I had to be seen and heard as a woman if I wanted my viewpoints to be heard. I could not just sit back in my office and just work hard if I wanted to influence change. I had to speak up and be visible. In advising women, I recommend that they sit at the table, raise their hands, and speak up.

Having supervisors with solid reputations as good managers and mentors is important to grow professionally. I often told my colleagues, especially women and my mentees, to do some research on the management style of the supervisors before accepting assignments. It is also acceptable to ask to interview them as they interview you for a job. A supportive, professionally secure and caring supervisor can help make your career. I worked for some of the best supervisors and am thankful for that. From my woman supervisors, I learned how to navigate and succeed in the predominately male dominated environment.

I tell my woman colleagues that networking is important. By habit, I am not a networker and often thought it was a waste of time. I believed that my work should speak for itself. However, over time, I learned that just like raising my hand and speaking up, having advocates who look out for you and know your work is an asset. Looking back on my career, I realized how a colleague who knew of my work and reputation came through for me. My first two jobs were on the recommendation of a friend who had worked with me and knew me professionally. My first senior level position was on the recommendation of a colleague and a friend who had seen me function at a previous post and was convinced that my management style was the right one for the position. She convinced her superiors and advocated for me. So, I encourage women to not shy away from networking. But be selective about who you network with and make sure they have your best interest at heart.

I was hoping by now that the world would be at a different and an equal place for women. Although many improvements have been made in my lifetime, they have been far too slow. I learned from my mother that women could achieve what men can, but I have seen that old attitudes still prevail, making progress slower and often difficult. I learned in my career that change takes time. I am hoping that by the time my eight-year-old grandnieces grow up they will not need to fight as hard as my generation had to and achieve what they want to professionally and personally.

The Women of My Family

Raminder Kaur

One cold December evening in Madison, Wisconsin, I entered my walk-in closet to get dressed. The six-by-eight-foot closet has a small chest of drawers with my jewelry boxes and other knickknacks positioned on top. The chest is covered by an ikat fabric from Uzbekistan. On the right are shelves. On one shelf, I have placed my multi-colored woolen skirts. I picked up a black and white skirt. I felt its warmth and a memory flashed in my mind.

My mother sits under a mango tree that spreads out lush and green, with unripe mangoes dangling; she is knitting a sweater. A basket filled with green and blue yarn is at her feet, and her two cats lazily lounge on the second chair next to her. The year is 1976. My father is the vice chancellor of the Punjab Agriculture University in Ludhiana, India. My parents live in a large house suitable for hosting university events. The garden has mango, peaches, and other fruit trees in the far corner. Red and yellow roses line the other three sides of the yard with seasonal flowers mixed in.

My mother started knitting as a teenager when she had time on her hands during her school vacations. She taught herself to make sweaters, blankets, socks, and caps. She knitted sweaters for everyone in the family. She knitted all the time. She even knitted in movie theaters, in the car, when she was not driving. She carries her bag full of wool and needles wherever she moves her sitting place in the house. Once settled, she pulls out what she is knitting and starts to knit. Her favorite place in her house is the lobby. It is the first room you enter when you come into the house. The lobby or foyer is centrally located, and she can see everyone in the house going about their business. The lobby is also the place where family members often sit and chat and have tea. My mother is like a permanent presence on the sofa facing the entry door in the lobby.

I have many pictures of my mother knitting. In one, she is sitting on a chair in front of a balcony opening on the La Rambla on a vacation in Barcelona. In another, she is in my living room in Yerevan, facing the balcony from which we could see Mt. Ararat. When she traveled to visit family and friends, her knitting paraphernalia traveled with her. Her knitting habit was a frequent conversational topic during our family get-togethers.

"Knitting is good for my aging hands," she would say as she grew older. "It keeps my mind occupied, and I don't have to think of stuff." She was referring to the grief she felt first for her father's death, then her husband's (my father), then her only grandson, and then her only son (my brother). The rhythmic movements of her hands and fingers soothed us as we sat together, with little to say, during the long, quiet, and dark evenings of grief after each of those deaths.

In the frigid winter of 2014, my mother visited me in Madison, where I had retired. She wanted a project.

"Please make me a woolen skirt that I can wear over my tights to keep me warm," I requested one day.

"What color would you like?" She was excited. Her knitting had found a renewed purpose.

I bought an indigo blue, two-shaded yarn and gave it to her. Two weeks later, she handed me the skirt. I received many compliments from friends and strangers. When I mentioned to my mother how much I appreciated the skirt and the compliments I received, she immediately wanted to make another.

"I have time on my hands. It will give me something to do during the winter," she said.

I bought yarn for two more skirts, a deep red one and a black and white one. She used an African motif for the black and white skirt, which perfectly blended in with my mostly black and white wardrobe. The red skirt created a much-needed contrast to all the black and white.

When she was back in India, she continued to knit skirts for me. Every time another family member visited India from the States, they brought back a skirt or two for me. As recently as 2021, when I visited India in January, she knitted me a deep blue and a red skirt. She said my other ones were getting old and that I should give them away. I have 22 skirts. I do not need any more skirts, but the pleasure I hear in her voice when I tell her about the many compliments that I receive stops me from telling her that I have enough.

My mother continued to knit more skirts, and I continued to add them to the shelf of my walk-in closet, knowing that a time would come when I would hold these skirts close to my face, wanting to feel her smell and touch.

Finally, that time came. I would have wished for a different way for her to leave this world but that was not to be. At the end of June 2023, she fell and broke her femur. She had surgery which was successful, and she was released from the hospital. I got to Chandigarh, India on July 12. Mother never gave up, as she had taught me to never give up. She was doing her physio and doing well, until one infection and the other took hold of her body. We took her back to the hospital on July 19, but after a trying time in the hospital which included twenty days in the ICU to manage her infections, we brought mother home.

My sister came from California and my mother was surrounded by love and her immediate small family. We had twenty-four-hour nursing help to make her as comfortable as possible. Mother's face would light up when her great granddaughters would come into her room. Mother recognized us through her oxygen mask and all her other medications that were prescribed to help her sleep at night. She was in no pain.

In mid-September she lost the ability to speak. Apparently, she had developed a growth in her throat which hindered her ability to speak. She would try to form words, and I could tell she wanted to tell us something, but we could not understand. She would want to write it, but no letters would form. That was frustrating for her, and she would turn her head away, finally giving up. Not being able to understand her, knowing that she wanted to say something or tell us something was extremely painful and heart wrenching for all of us.

One evening in mid-October sitting in her room, I was reading *The Longest Night* by Otto De Kat, a book about waiting, preparing to die, and being ready for it while remembering moments in life. I looked at my mother and wondered what she was experiencing, if she knew her end was near. Emma, the protagonist in the book, planned her death; my mother did not have that opportunity. I wish she had that choice. I wish I had asked her when she was able to talk as to how she wanted to go. I wish she had been able to say "goodbye." We each spent time alone with her, telling her we loved her, that we were sorry for some of the disagreements and arguments, asking her forgiveness. We comforted ourselves with the thought that she could hear us. When she took her last breath, she was surrounded by loved ones. Experts on death and dying tell me that is the best way to go, surrounded by loved ones and in one's own home. Why do their words not comfort me?

When I was very young, I thought my mother was the most beautiful women in the whole world. Her presence was all the security I needed. One day—it must have been around 1945, and I was three years old—she was in the kitchen cutting vegetables to cook for the evening meal. As she cut, I would pick one piece at a time from the platter and throw it on the ground. She waited for me to do this for a considerable amount of time asking me to stop a few times. Finally, I wore her patience down. Without getting angry, she picked me up and handed me over to someone else in the house and said, "She is bored; maybe she needs to go out and play." That is how I remember her, patient and considerate.

We then lived in a small rural village town with minimal facilities, such as household help, common in India, which my parents could not afford then. My mother did the cooking and all the major housework. The kitchen and the wood burning fire pitch was the old style "*chula*" on the ground and my mother would sit on a low stool to do much of the preparation and cooking. Occasionally she would feed a piece of wood to the burner to keep the fire going. I would often sit next to her, trying to help, but not really. The person she handed me over was Inder Singh a kindly man assigned to the government house that we lived in and who took care of the outdoor chores. I remember him picking me up, putting me on his bike and riding around the agricultural fields surrounding the village/town. My mother knew how much I enjoyed riding around the bike with Inder Singh and from that day on, it became our daily activity when my mother had to do her morning household tasks. I loved her for that understanding.

She recognized the need for me to be educated and talked my father into sending me to live with her father in New Delhi, a big city where there were better schools. She was firm about my education and always believed that girls can achieve whatever they wish and want to. I often wondered if her passion to see me and my sister get an education was grounded in her not being able to complete her schooling. She had to quit school to take care of her siblings when her mother fell sick with a chronic disease. I never heard her regret that decision but just accepted it as a duty.

My mother was also ahead of her times. She learned how to drive and loved it. My father was never a good driver, so my mother drove us around as needed. Her belief that women are equal and can achieve whatever they aspire to, unique in her times. She was an avid reader. She also did more of the traditional tasks like knitting and embroidery. And she took music and singing lessons. She loved travelling. Being around her was like being in the presence of a person who was perfect. An exemplary role model to follow.

Despite the personal grief she endured due to all the deaths of those close to her, she was a stable force in the family. Her mantras have helped me during my life: stay focused on the task at hand, stay mentally busy, take responsibility, don't indulge in self-pity, focus on the wellbeing of others, and never give up hope and above all be kind and forgiving. I often wonder what choices she would have made if she had been able to finish her education and not get married at the age of fourteen.

In November I returned to Madison, a month after mother's transition from this world and once the cultural and religious ceremonies were completed. One day, I entered my closet. All my skirts were neatly folded as I had left them waiting to be worn. It was not cold enough in Madison when I had left for India. I touched each of them, sensing her moving hands with each stitch.

My mother leaves behind girls and women in the family who in their own ways are being strong, resilient and loving as they manage and live their lives and make their stories. Her great grandson is a gentle soul and supportive of woman in the family. Her grandchildren and great grandchildren called her *Dayia,* paternal grandmother and *Nani,* maternal grandmother.

Satinder (boona)

My sister boona is the bravest person I know. In 1969, at the age of twenty-four, she left India to go to South Vietnam during the war with the International Voluntary Services and Committee of

Responsibility to work with napalm burned children and women's health.

"The time in Vietnam allowed me to start thinking about the status of women and children in a patriarchal world. A world full of war where women and children became collateral damage," she tells me. "Being a woman for me is about love, empathy, spirituality, activism and social justice."

This commitment to social justice and equity led her to Star King School for the Ministry in Berkeley, California (a Unitarian Universalist School) which led her to Berkeley Hill Project now Building Opportunities for Self-Sufficiency (BOSS) where she started as a cook for the homeless and later served as its Executive Director from 1976 to 2013.

Whether speaking truth to power at public meetings, lobbying furiously for funding for community-based organizations and collaboratives at the local, state and federal levels, her unstoppable voice has continued to work actively for civil and human rights with focus on urban and rural refugees. She is best known for her work with homeless populations.

"I emulate our mother and her vision of a just world," she says. "I am bestowed by the teachings of my mother and the other women in my family as they raised me, and I developed the ability to filter what worked for them and how I could apply their teachings to my purpose in life as a woman."

In recognition of boona's work, a week is dedicated in her name in Alameda County, California, and a day in the city of Berkeley.

Chloe

My mother's great granddaughter, Chloe, is a storyteller and a story maker. She has a diary with her all the time. When she was four years old, her stories started with "Once upon a time" and ended with "lived happily ever after." She is strong-minded like her *dayia* and knows what she wants at the young age of eight years old.

During the first five years of Chloe's life, I spent considerable time with her. She lived with her parents on the first floor of the condo building I live in. I took her to tennis lessons, watched and played with her when her parents were at work.

I played her favorite games; first it was the characters from *Frozen*—she was always Elsa and I was Anna. Later, she moved on to the LOL doll characters. In between there was *Cinderella* and *Aladdin* and many more stories that she would role play with me. Chloe always chose who would play which character and which scene we would dramatize from the books her mother read to her or the videos she watched.

I loved it when her mother would call, and I would hear Chloe asking in the background if she could come up. "Of course, you can," I would say. I could never say, "No." Looking back at those times, I can understand the joy of grandparents when they have access to their grandkids. Chloe's grandparents lived on two different continents. Her father's parents in Berkeley and her mother's parents Nanu and Nani in Chandigarh, India. Chloe saw them during the holidays, but I had the privilege of spending the extended time with her. That time with her over the first years of her life will remain my most treasured and precious memories, forever.

One afternoon during our play time, Chloe asked me to tell her a story about her birth. "Call me Chimku in the story," she said. She was curious as to why she was born in India. So, I told her this story:

"Once upon a time, four years ago, a little girl called Chimku was in her mommy's tummy. She snuggled up as close as she could get to her mommy and felt warm and cozy. She usually slept most of the day and night to the rhythm of her mommy's heartbeat. Sometimes she wanted to stretch and then she would hear "ouch" from her mommy, and she would curl up again to cause her mommy no discomfort. Chimku was happy doing nothing.

"Then, one day, she heard her mommy and daddy talking loudly, making plans to leave. Someone was sick, she did not know who. A few days later her mommy and dada were on a plane to India. Chimku did not know what and where India was—she felt a change in her mommy. She was unhappy and cried sometimes. Chimku reached out her little hand and touched her mommy's tommy from inside and softly said "Mommy all will be fine, I am here." The plane ride was no fun, up and down, Chimku felt her heart was going to come out of her body—but her mommy always kept her hand on her tummy, which made Chimku feel safe.

"When they reached India, there were lots of new voices. Chimku did not understand what they were saying. Everyone was talking at the same time. Chimku just wanted to sleep and sometimes poop. Chimku was growing fast and felt squeezed in. She needed more space and kicked her mommy to let her know. All she got was a pat on her mommy's tummy. No extra room was made for Chimku.

"One night, she heard her mommy say, 'It's time, let's go to the hospital.' Chimku did not want to go to a new house. So, she kicked some more, which only made her mommy say—"Quick, quick. Chimku is coming". Coming from where? Chimku thought, I am already here.

"There was no comfort for Chimku after that—she heard loud big people chatter, saw bright lights, and then she felt as if she were being lifted out of the sea of her mommy's tummy by two large hands.

"Nooooo," Chimku screamed.

"Then she landed on something soft.

"There was a lot of fuss. Chimku was a little disoriented and wanted to crawl back into her mommy's warm and safe tummy. But then she was in the arms of her mama, and dada was close by, and she closed her eyes and was happy. The end."

"No," said Chloe. "I want more."

"And they lived happily ever after," I added.

"But—who was sick?" Chloe asked.

"Your grandpa, *Nanu*." There was a moment of silence.

"He died and became a star—right? and that is why I was born in India!" she finally said.

"Yes, that is right," I said.

She was silent for a while and then said, "Let's play Frozen. You are Anna."

Her maternal grandfather, (*Nanu*) was struggling with an autoimmune disease and was in the hospital, the reason for the trip to India for Chloe's parents. Unfortunately, he did not meet Chloe. But her mother kept his memory alive through pictures and his stories. When Chloe asked where he went after he died, her mother would say, "In the stars." To this day, when Chloe looks up at the sky at night, she often says, "So *Nanu* is up there with the stars."

Chloe also is a storyteller and keeps a diary and loves singing songs like Price Tag, Die with a Smile. None that I know off. Here is one of her songs she wrote and performed for me two years ago.

> You are who you are, la,la,la
> You should not hide who you are,
> If you hide who you are—you will lose,
> If you hide who you are—you will isolate who you are,
> You are who you are. La,la,la

"Now your turn," she said when finished.

When I came up with nothing, she said, "I won."

Chloe likes challenges, and every game is a competition. When she does not win, she says, "Never give up—try, try again." And, at that moment, I think of my mother and her mantra of never giving up.

Ava

My mother's second great-granddaughter, Ava, is a bit goofy and funny and a teaser, working behind the scenes, even at the age of six. A friend visiting the family called her a "wood sprite"—mischievous and hiding things. According to folklore, a sprite is much like a fairy that lives within and maintains an individual tree. In the movie *Avatar*, wood sprites are seeds from the Tree of Souls and the Na'vi revere them and consider them bearers of omen and signs of sanctity.

If there is anything missing of her mother's, such as keys, phone, her small purse—she asks Ava, because she knows that Ava quietly hides things when no one is around and has hidden it in a safe place. Ava is always working behind the scenes, so it seems. When I see her look at me, I often wonder, what is she planning now, what is she thinking to do to get my attention.

Ava and her mother often have ongoing conversations, such as this one during a plane trip:

Ava: "Mom where am I?"

Mom: "Ava where are you?"

Ava: "Right behind you, girl."

Mom: "Stop making that funny noise while chewing your food."

Ava pats her mother on the back. "Calm down girl. All is fine."

Ava on the phone with her mother: "Mom, where are you?"

Mom: "At the store."

Ava: "Did you buy me a gift?"

Mom: "No."

Ava: "My life is over."

Her mother bursts out laughing.

One day during my visit to Chandigarh, where Ava lives, we were in a rickshaw coming home from the library. She was singing and making funny comments about the people passing by. When we passed the Sikh *Gurdwara* (temple), she got all serious and asked me if we could stop. "I want to make a wish," she said.

We stopped and went in. With no other words exchanged, she covered her head with a scarf from the basket placed outside the entrance to the room with the sacred book. She walked to the altar and knelt there for a few minutes. I stayed back at the door to give her time. Then, we walked back to the rickshaw. She said she had wished for something dear to her. I did not ask what she had wished for. Sitting there in front of me, she had her chin up. She was no longer interested in chatting. She looked out at the world now with a look of determination. At that moment, I thought of my mother's determined face so many years ago when my dad had died. Mother stood in the reception line, greeting visitors who had come to share their condolences, she held Ava's mother, who was three years old, in her arms, and accepted everyone's words of comfort and sympathy with a determined look. A look which said, I am ready to face reality.

She told us that all will be well. Ava sitting across from me in the rickshaw had that look.

Sukhmani

Sukhmani, my mother's granddaughter, is an artist and an animal lover. I asked her what she learned from my mother as a woman.

"I admire her perseverance, how she takes care of herself and us—waiting for us late at nights when we got home late. Her nurturing nature and love of books. Her knowledge of politics, religion, house stuff—she knows so much. I have learned patience; hopefully I will learn perseverance too. She has gone through so much and still is positive and continues to take care of so many people. She is always calm and content. I want to be like that. Being just twenty percent of her is a challenge. She has a routine and balance to how she does things. I am all over the place."

But Sukhmani is not all over the place. She incorporates some of what she admired and learned from her grandmother into her life while she recovered from her dad's and her grandmother's death. She was very close to my mother, who was her primary caretaker when she was young. Her dad was her security blanket. Her six poodles and her horse, Mira, have helped her through her grief and loss. She says, "My animals have saved me."

She is in the process of building a farmhouse where she can be with nature and her animals and continue to discover herself.

Sukhmani takes immense pleasure in her conversations with her daughter Ava. I can see them being friends and enjoying each other as Ava grows up.

Sukhmani tells me, "Being a woman is not just about managing a house, taking care of your family, taking care of work and business, but how you grow on a personal level. Being sheltered and protected all my life and then losing my father .... I had to grow up overnight and take on responsibilities about which I had no clue. Each year since then has been a learning experience, facing new challenges and then overcoming them by finding solutions. I grew up as a person and as a woman. People around me expected me to be strong and move on, which is not bad advice and what I learned from my grandmother. But sometimes I did not want to be such a strong person and wanted to give up. Then I see my six-year-old walking by me, and I know that I need to be an example for her future by not just telling her what to do but being present and with my actions to see and learn as she grows up as a girl to be the woman she will one day be. That right now is who I am as a woman."

Bani

Bani, my mother's other granddaughter, is acutely aware of her constant search for herself.

"As a woman growing up in India, I was lucky to have strong role models in my family that allowed me to choose my own path. My father gave me the space and confidence to make decisions and learn life lessons with courage. While my mother provided the humility to live life with grace and gratitude. When I lost my dad, it was almost as if I lost my identity and had to start re-building who I am. My aunt stepped in a big way and unknowingly, I was ready for the challenges ahead.

Ironically, within a month of losing my father, I also became a mother. It was difficult to manage my grief and joy within. I began to spend a lot of nights with *Dayia* as she helped me with my newborn. I watched her channel her loss, turning her emotions into so much love and care for the future whom she held in her arms. From her, I learned about continuing to move forward, not being held back by fear. To be the woman, I am.

It's been almost eight years and at 40 looking back I am certain that I am exactly where I'm meant to be in my life, career, as a mother, daughter, aunt, niece and sister. I have finally accepted myself as a strong woman even though sometimes I have to fight twice as hard to succeed. Now, I work even harder to equip my daughter with the tools to work hard, be resilient, be kind and compassionate and to achieve her dreams.

I struggled with my dad's death, until one day, I found some acceptance. I realized grief will stay with me forever. I wrote about these feelings and shared it hoping other daughters and mothers could learn from my pain and experience:

It's taken a while but writing this below and sharing it gave me some peace.

"Four years ago, today was the worst day of my life. My dad died. And with him I lost a father, a friend, a mentor and a big part of my identity. Here I was nine months pregnant, cremating him in absolute numbness with no clue what I was going to do. For the last year all I had heard from him was "don't worry" and "everything's going to be fine." How the f… was I not supposed to worry he was dead? My daughter would never get to see him. What about his legacy? What am I going to do? So many questions were racing through my mind while I felt deep, deep pain.

Three weeks later my beautiful baby girl was born, and she rescued our family. She helped us balance our grief and deep loss with joy and made us remember that we were still very alive! And I knew what I had to do, I had to move forward for her and be happy no matter how I felt.

Today, I may not have all my answers and think every day what it would be like if he was around to help me make my decisions or give me a big hug, I would be the one to tell him dad it's all ok. We are okay! Once I realized that my dad's legacy is not so much about what he did or what he wanted me to do but more about the choices I make upholding the values he taught me and how gracefully I live my life, the more peace I feel. We (my sister and I) are his legacy.

I still have deep grief, but I also have a lot to be grateful for. The pain is less intense, and I can finally breathe and remember him. He would be happy to see me thrive, be independent and raise a strong and kind child. Above all I feel his strength and see his fearless spirit in my daughter. Papa I will always feel your void in my life but am so glad I get to be your daughter every day."

PART IV

Home

*"You can have more than one home.
You can carry your roots with you,
and decide where they grow"*

Henning Mankell

What Is Home?

On one early fall day of October 2023, I walked out of the bedroom to the kitchen, quietly shutting the door behind me as Jeff was still asleep. I went to the kitchen and turned on the tea kettle. I reached into the closet and randomly got a cup from the shelf. I added a G-tips black tea bag. I added sugar. I added a cardamon and a piece of clove. Once the water boiled, I poured it in my cup, added milk and let the tea bag soak for a few minutes. I carried my cup to the sofa where I sat facing the window. It was a little cool. I reached for the blanket that my mother had knitted which I kept on the sofa, to cover myself. "I am at home," I said to myself. But then I wondered, what is home? And I thought of all the places that I had lived in—had they all been home?

My father was in the civil service, so we moved often. Between the age of five and seven, we moved to three cities. I went to school in Delhi and stayed at one place until I was fifteen. After living with my parents during high school and college, I went back to Delhi for graduate studies. When I got married, I moved to several countries where my husband was posted. After we divorced, I moved to the US and lived in Boston. Working with USAID, I moved every couple of years and finally settled in Madison, Wisconsin. By the time I retired I had lived in between forty to fifty houses.

I asked my mother as I grew up about how I adjusted and what I did. As a toddler, she said that I had no attachment to dolls or favorite toys. When we moved to a new place, I would find a corner or some space in the house and would arrange the space with whatever toys or books or anything else that I found interesting, such as pots and pans and her books. That space is where she said she would find me often busy with arranging and rearranging my things.

I first remember the need to find my own space in the Faridkot house in 1947. I was five years old. I would sit in a corner next to the open kitchen in the courtyard where the temporary kitchen was located to feed and serve hot tea to the refugees who were passing to and back from the border. I would linger in a corner watching for hours. I wanted to help but was too young to go near the fire. I liked that space in that corner watching the activity for hours. I felt safe.

After six months, when we moved to Patiala, my mother brought home two puppies, and they took over my life. They took over the need for a special place. The space where puppies spent their time became my space and where I felt most comfortable. I don't remember being anywhere else in the house.

When I was six, we moved to Nabha. The house was originally a government guest house for VIP visitors. Later it was turned into individual apartments for government civil service officers. The building covered a block, and a common verandah connected four family units. There were five or six other kids all younger than me living in the compound. I took over organizing our play time which involved a space on the roof of one of the units. Each one of us took our favorite items, spread a plastic mat on the floor and made our homes. We dragged two benches over, put a blanket on top and called it our shelter. My mother told me that she would find me there even after the kids went home.

In my grandfather's house, when I went to Delhi for schooling, I made a space next to my bed and organized my favorite stuffed animal, a picture of my parents, and a small music box that my mother gave me. My bed was next to a window from which I could see the world go by. After school, I would sit looking out of the window onto the street. I would immerse myself in the activity of the street. I created a game where I would pretend to follow a car or someone on foot and imagine their lives—who they were, where they lived, where they worked. I gave them names and hobbies. I gave some of them important positions and some got to be just regular working people if they were on a bike or walking. I imagined people in cars had important roles. That space became my safe space.

With every move, I remember carrying my paraphernalia and creating a space of my own in a corner, next to a window or any other place. A chair with a small rug for my feet was enough to give me that feeling of my space. A space where I want to spend my time and feel my own. Later when I was working with USAID and we moved often, I would, as soon as my household affects were delivered, immediately open a few boxes, take some books, a family picture and few other items and walk around the house to find a space for these few items to mark as my space where I would put my feet up and read. When I was in Kabul living in a *hooch*, I went to the market, organized at the military base on the very first weekend, and bought two rugs to cover the metal floor. I bought colorful hand-woven cushions filled with cotton and made a small sitting area in the corner. I hung a colorful Indian scarf on the bathroom door to highlight the entrance.

I printed a few family pictures and taped them on the wall next to the bed. I created my space and felt ready for my work and to learn about the country. Our work hours were long in Kabul and no matter what hour I walked in my hootch and sank on my soft cushions, I was enveloped in the warmth of my space, and I felt at home.

Even in the smallest places, I found my space. Jeffrey was amused when on a long train trip from Wisconsin to California, I unfolded a small table next to the window in our sleeper compartment and on it arranged my book, my journal, my art supplies, and a small carved box. There was a small chair beside the window. For three nights and two days while I crossed the continent, that space was my home.

While sipping my tea in my Madison condo, I realized that for me, home is where I felt safe. For me, in each house, in each country, once I had my special space to return to, I felt free to explore, learn, and experience my life in each new place.

Walking through the Walker Museum in Minneapolis I saw a plaque that read, "This must be the place: Home is more than just a place on a map. Relationships, memories, feelings and politics are all part of this complex subject.

October 1984

On October 31, 1984, I was at the New York airport returning home to Arlington, Virginia, where I was living in between short-term assignments, when the news broke that Indira Ghandhi, the prime minister of India, had been assassinated. At first there was no mention of the assailant. During the plane ride, I had no more news, but my anxiety remained high. I kept repeating to myself, please don't let it be a Sikh. As soon I entered my apartment, I turned on the TV and learned that her Sikh bodyguards had shot the prime minister.

India had been in the news since April 1984 when a separatist movement by Sikhs for greater autonomy and a Sikh state started and soon was termed as an insurgency against the government. The Blue Star Operation was launched by the government to counter the movement. As part of the operation, the Indian army was positioned to enter the Golden Temple where many of the activists, including its leader, had taken shelter. For days there were negotiations and discussions, but finally the Indian army entered the temple, considered the most holy place for the Sikh community. There were casualties on both sides and the assault also damaged the temple's structure. There were calls for revenge. Indira Ghandi, the prime minister had authorized the military action, which created a strong reaction from the Sikh community in India and around the world. Those were intense days. Then she was assassinated.

I was nervous, I knew there would be retaliation. I had the TV on all the time. Within days, the anti-Sikh riots started. What followed were horrific scenes on TV. Across India, especially north India, where the majority of the Sikhs live. Gangs, mostly Hindu, killed innocent Sikhs. I saw mobs putting tires around people, spraying gasoline on them, and then igniting them, burning them alive. I saw scenes of Sikhs being dragged out of their houses by the mobs and beaten and killed. These were my people, and the Indian government did nothing for days. The burnings and killings continued. There were rumors that a high-level politician in the Indian government said, "Let them (the Hindus) get their anger out." The Indian government let the riots continue for days; independent reports said that 8,000 to 17,000 innocent people were killed—just because they were from the Sikh community and faith.

That event changed something deep inside me. Besides being disappointed at the lack of timely action by the government, I was sad and depressed at what was happening to my community. I was afraid for my family back in India. It triggered memories of 1947. I could not sleep. I could not eat. My sadness started to turn into anger and rage.

I started to question my identity. I had been a US citizen and had been living in the States since 1973. I was proud of my Indian identity. I liked wearing my Indian dresses on occasions and to work. I liked to cook Indian food for my friends. But for days after, I could not bear the thought that the Indian government, the country in which I was born and did nothing to protect my people.

Then, I stopped wearing the sari. I was so angry that I did not want to be seen as an Indian. I cut my long hair even shorter. I stopped cooking and eating Indian food at home. When people asked me where I was from, I would tell them Washington, DC, or Ann Arbor where I had done my graduate and post graduate work. I could not say that I was from India.

Over time, my anger softened. I am proud to be of Indian origin, but more so of Sikh heritage.

I continue to visit India to see my family. But I feel like an outsider when I am there. This experience of feeling like an outsider in a country I was born in has freed me from pressure to identify myself with a place. I feel free from any culturally defined parameters of a country or religion. I feel that I can make my own identity where I am. Being free of any cultural baggage makes it possible for me to adapt, adjust, and make all the places I have lived in—my home.

A Place to Be

When I retired, Jeff and I bought a condo on Williamson Street in Madison. I thought this is it. My place. I can finally establish roots and make friends and never have to move again. My two-bedroom condo is a place where we entertain friends and family. We furnished it with our collection of paintings, rugs, African masks and other mementoes we collected in our travels, reminding us of our life in the different parts of the world. But something was missing. As much as I loved being in our condo. I needed something more..

A few blocks from our condo there was a two-story blue building at 911 Williamson Street that I admired whenever I walked by it. I liked its structure and its history. It was built in 1896 for Frank G. Dickert and operated as a shoe store for nearly twenty years. The family had lived next door in a larger house. The ground floor, I am told, had been the shop with a small workshop to make the shoes upstairs. When I moved to Willy Street, it was a hemp store and sold bags, clothing and other items made from hemp. The high ceilings, old bronze hanging lights with globe shades, original hard wood floor that creaked in places, added to its charm. I would often walk in. I liked being inside this building.

One morning in early November 2012, I was walking to Wilson Street where I volunteered at a temporary office set up by the Obama campaign. With my hands in my pockets and my head down to avoid the bitter wind stinging my eyes, I walked fast. My backpack with my computer felt heavy with every step. For some reason, I paused in front of the blue building. I saw a FOR SALE sign in the window. I read and re-read the sign. I knew then that I wanted the building for my space.

I acquired the building in February 2013, and the hemp store manager decided to close his retail business. I was delighted. I could make it mine. I had a vision of a place where people could meet and have conversations. My years abroad in the foreign service in places where English was not the spoken language had left me longing to have more social contact and dialogue. As a US diplomat, I was somewhat careful of how I discussed issues. Now, I wanted to have free and open discussions without self-censorship. The rise in social media had left me wanting more in-person contact. I wanted to create an environment which was warm and welcoming for all. In my mind I saw people sitting comfortably on sofas and lounge chairs holding cups of warm tea or glasses of wine, relaxing and conversing. I also saw this place as somewhere where I could reflect and figure out what my life would be like after my official retirement. I was not ready to retire in the traditional sense of the word. I wanted to continue to be engaged and grow and keep learning and experiencing and giving back to the community.

Painting the walls and furnishing the place became critical. I settled on a warm purple for the left wall with Van Gogh sunflower yellow toward the far left, which brightened the room immediately. On the Van Gogh yellow wall, I hung my photographs and certificates and awards. I wanted people to know me through this place. Every time I walk in, I am struck by the warmth of the yellow wall.

On the right side I chose a deep red followed by grey for the door and the window trimming to create a contrast with the red. I furnished the place with a comfortable sofa and working chairs. For the sofa, I used cushions designed by my niece from old silk saris my mother had worn and other materials she carefully selected from different parts of India giving the place a family feel. A carpenter friend made me a conference table from an old door he found in an abandoned mansion in a small town in Wisconsin. Another friend offered benches and an antique secretary desk, adding to the old character of the building.

The floors needed covering. I used a deep maroon, slightly faded old red rug made from natural dyes that I had bought during my first tour in Almaty, Kazakhstan. It is a tribal rug made in 1960; the date is woven into the rug. I was told that the rug was made by a mother for her two daughters and the names of the daughters are woven into one corner of the rug. I added an Armenian blue runner that I had bought in Nagorno Karabakh, a disputed enclave over which numerous conflicts have erupted between Armenia and Azerbaijan. I wanted it there as a reminder of the conflicts in the world. Under the conference table, I placed a bright red Kazak carpet with flower motifs, a carpet purchased during my second tour in Almaty in 2017 and woven by hand in a factory with traditional designs, but with artificial dyes which were more easily available. I wanted to show the continuity of culture and tradition adapting to modern technologies.

The place needed a name. I was enjoying a glass of wine with a friend, the owner of a local clothing boutique called Change at the corner of Baldwin and Williamson. We were talking about her business and life and what we could do to promote woman-owned businesses. I felt so right in being in the place having those conversations. Suddenly I said, "A Place to Be, that is what I will call my conversation place."

I found myself spending more and more time at A Place to Be. I did my assignments there for a creative writing course I was taking at the University of Wisconsin. I moved in an upright piano I had bought in Armenia. I started taking piano lessons. The space gave me inspiration. I felt calm and reflective.

In 2016, I started work on writing my mother's life history. While working on this project, I found solace in the place, and it prompted me to think more about my memories and my work and my life experiences.

For the community, it has become known as a place where people can pursue their interests and hold discussions about topics for which they are passionate about. I started the women's business network which met to connect and help expand each other's businesses. The death café, a part of a worldwide movement to talk about death and dying, meet at A Place to Be. A writers' group use the place to coach and motivate writers. A parent group promoting nonviolent communication found the place perfect for their sensitive subject matter. A psychedelic group started to meet once a month. A workshop on forgiveness meets once a month. Many other small startups trying to be heard and make a difference meet at A Place to Be. I was pleased that I was giving something back to the community.

I closed the place during COVID and used A Place to Be for myself and wrote my first book. It became my special space where I could open old letters and boxes full of pictures, see my life spread out in front of me, and to piece it together, postcard by post card, letter by letter.

A Place to Be made me a writer. I never want to let it go, but I know someday I will have to. It is just a place, and I will need to leave it behind one day. I am hoping that those using the place in the future will feel it's energy, warmth, and welcoming spirit to help learn, grow, heal, and accept others, no matter how different. It has helped me grow and learn more about myself and my life in ways that I did not know before.

Acknowledgements

Thank you to my spouse Jeffrey Wright for helping me stay the course during the difficult time, after my mother's death, when I felt empty and silent inside and could find no words. To the women in my family who shared their stories. To my friends, who were there for me when I was grieving for my mother and trying to finish the book.

I appreciate my writing coach, Christopher Chambers, for his assistance with the successful completion of this book. Without his support, I might not have stayed with the project. And of course, to my publisher and all the staff at Calumet Editions who helped to make the book a reality, and to my editor Susan.

Throughout my career, I had the opportunity to work with outstanding Ambassadors and USAID staff. I am grateful to them. Each one of them influenced me professionally and I learned much from them. Thank you for serving our country and for your support to me as I did my part in a small way to make a difference.

I thank all who reviewed sections of this book and provided invaluable feedback to make it a better read.

Some material in *A Place to Be* appears in Dr. Cheema, Jatinder: Oral History, Interviewed by Ann Van Dusen, Foreign Affairs Oral History Collection: Foreign Assistance Series, Association for Diplomatic Studies and Training, Arlington, VA, adst.org.

About the Author

Jantinder Cheema (nickname Gud) has lived and served in multiple countries managing and overseeing development programs. She worked in Central Asia, Armenia, South Asia, Afghanistan, and countries in Africa.

Born in 1942 in India, she witnessed history in the making as the subcontinent of India was being divided into the separate countries of India and Pakistan. As a daughter of a civil service officer, moving frequently and living in different places was an integral part of her upbringing.

In 1974, Cheema moved to the United States for graduate and post-graduate studies at the University of Michigan, Ann Arbor. After graduating, she worked with International Organizations as a development consultant and in 1991 joined the United States Agency for International Development as a career Foreign Service Officer. She reached the ranks of a Senior Foreign Service Officer before finally retiring in 2012.

During her career, Cheema sought volunteer opportunities, and participated in forums to speak to women and young professionals on leadership and career enhancement. After retirement, she founded "A Place to Be" a salon for creative conversation and dialogue, in Madison, Wisconsin, where she currently lives with her husband. She continues to actively engage in local development issues.

Cheema has a master's degree in Social Work, a masters in Public Health and a PhD in Social Sciences.

www.ingramcontent.com/pod-product-compliance
Lightning Source LLC
Chambersburg PA
CBHW020226170426
43201CB00007B/335